DIRK BOGARDE

RANK OUTSIDER

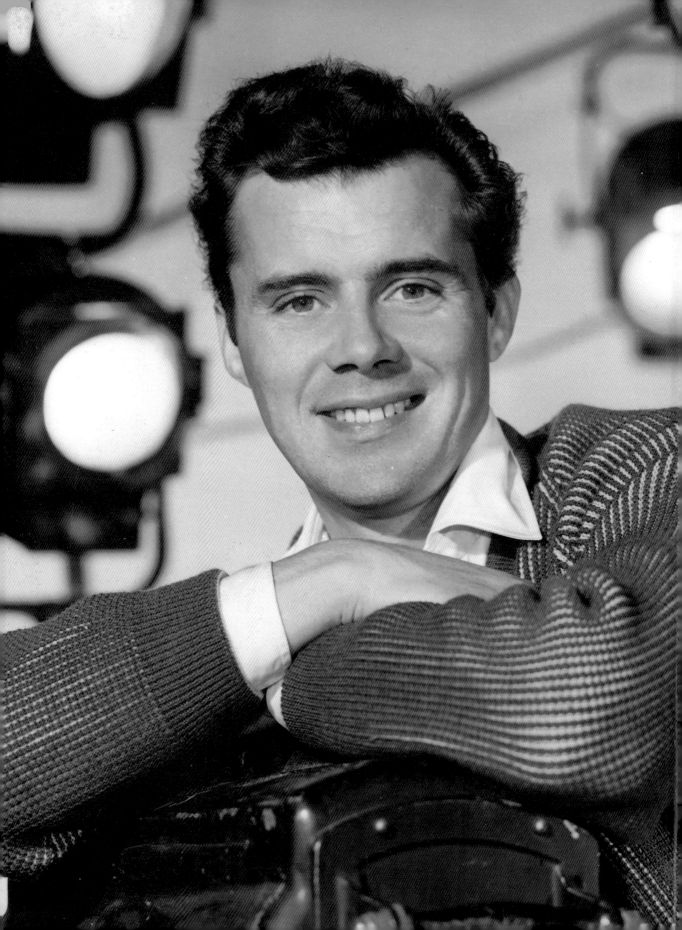

DIRK BOGARDE

RANK OUTSIDER

SHERIDAN MORLEY

BLOOMSBU

FOR RUTH, WITHOUT WHOM THIS BOOK WOULD NOT BE A BOOK

First published in Great Britain in 1996
Bloomsbury Publishing Plc, 2 Soho Square, London W1V 6HB

PICTURE SOURCES
British Museum, London
Camera Press, London
Camera Press, London/photos Peter Mitchell, Eva Sereny,
Christopher Smith, Terry Smith
Corbis UK
Joel Finler Collection, London
Harvard Theatre Collection, Massachusetts
Hulton Deutsch, London
Kobal Collection, London
Pictorial Press, London
Rex Features, London
Times Newspapers Limited
© Bob Willoughby 1996

BFI Stills Posters and Designs, London, with acknowledgement to: Action/SFP, Alfa,
Allied Film Makers, Anglo-Amalgamated/Warner-Pathe, Associated British/Spring Bok,
Avco Embassy, BHE Productions, Bavaria Atelier/SFP/Geria, British Lion, Clea/Solyfic Eurisma/Little
Bear/Avenue, Ealing, Embassy, Frobisher/Eros, Gainsborough/Sydney Box,
London Independent Producers, MGM, MGM/Comet, Paramount, Pegaso/Italnoleggio/Praesidens/Eichberg,
Rank, Twentieth Century-Fox, United Artists, Warner Brothers/Sascha.

Every reasonable effort has been made to acknowledge the ownership of copyrighted
photographs included in this volume. Any errors that have inadvertently occurred will be
corrected in subsequent editions provided notification is sent to the publisher.

A CIP catalogue record for this book
is available from the British Library

ISBN 0 7475 2563 3

10 9 8 7 6 5 4 3 2 1

Picture research by Juliet Brightmore
Designed by Bradbury and Williams
Designer: Bob Burroughs
Originated by Vimnice Printing Press, Hong Kong
Printed and bound by Bath Press, Great Britain

CONTENTS

PROLOGUE

'I love the camera

and it seems to love

me. Not always very

much, admittedly, but

we have managed to

remain good friends.'

The British cinema, like the Hollywood he has always distrusted even more strongly, has traditionally remained somewhat uneasy about Dirk Bogarde; local film stars of his generation were not supposed to write seven volumes of seriously good autobiography and five novels. Nor were they supposed to live abroad, unless in California, and still less were they expected to turn up in the better art-house movies of European directors.

When interviewed, they were expected whenever possible to be enthusiastic, hopeful and graceful about the state of their careers, and to express surprise and considerable gratitude for the way that these had panned out over the years. They were not supposed to be hugely intelligent or cynically witty, advocate euthanasia or remain generally depressed and somewhat cranky abut the social and professional ways of a world from which they seemed to wish to withdraw into an almost total isolation.

But then Dirk Bogarde is not your average movie star. This makes it all the more surprising that this book, though in no way intended to be his life story (which he has already written rather better than most), should be the first critical study of a brief stage and a long screen career stretching back more than fifty years.

As a nation we tend to breed great stage stars who then sometimes take to the movies in later life, as did Olivier and Gielgud and Redgrave; we seldom breed great movie stars, and when we do they usually seem to end up in some kind of internal or geographic exile, painfully aware that their own country has never quite managed to give them the credit that would have been

OPPOSITE: DAZZLED BY *THE HIGH BRIGHT SUN* (1965). BELOW: THE BEARD WAS FOR *HUNTED* (1952) AND HE HATED IT.

theirs had they stayed in the wings and on the stage of the Old Vic.

If you were looking for a stage actor of Bogarde's generation who shared his utter belief in the importance of the work and of rejecting any unworthy scripts, then you would probably have to look to Paul Scofield. But if you were looking for his only true rival as a postwar British film star, then you would, I think, look to James Mason. Both men were often profoundly unhappy with the Anglo-American studio system and what they perceived as its hidebound casting traditions and what these had done to their careers; both fled the England they once loved, to live not always easily or happily abroad, and both knew something special about the camera

AS THE KING OF THE TURF WITH KATHLEEN RYAN IN HIS FIRST FILM, *ESTHER WATERS* (1948).

that it had to see you *think* as well as act.

Both men would have been infinitely happier working in the European cinema, where directors and writers were reckoned as important as actors, and both men were distrusted by audiences at home precisely because they were moody, thoughtful and utterly unwilling to come out of the same corner of the screen more than once. Before the term acquired its pornographic overtones, they stood for adult cinema in an industry still dominated by overgrown schoolboys.

Above all, they were a constant challenge not only to themselves but also to those working with them: refusing ever to accept that film acting was somehow inferior to live theatre, they also refused to make it easy on themselves or those around them. They simply wanted the best at a time when English-speaking movies seldom strove for that kind of excellence or art. And they paid a high price: Bogarde's entire domestic career can be viewed as the history of the British cinema's faltering attempts to come of age.

As far back as 1948, when *Esther Waters* gave him, accidentally as it turned out, his first starring role, he was playing a thoroughly bad lot rather than the heroic Latin lover earmarked for him by a Hollywood film company with a sharp eye for a new face. Only a year later *The Blue Lamp*, the film that gave birth to *Dixon of Dock Green*, cemented his reputation as the sexiest villain in England. He got his first raves for this anti-hero; the critic in *The Times* enthused, 'Dirk Bogarde, as a

representative of the new type of criminal ... gives an admirable performance.'

There was already a brooding quality in the dark good looks, a restlessness just under the surface of each performance, as if an explosion was being suppressed just by good manners.

The producer Betty Box is an intelligent woman who was always on the lookout for substance as well as style. She recognized this dangerous quality in Bogarde and knew that if it could be wedded to comedy she would have something special. The 'something special' in her terms was in *Doctor in the House*, a smash hit comedy which spawned a string of hugely successful sequels. Their very success threatened his dramatic aspirations but at least Bogarde was finding out what kind of film actor he could be. The *Doctor* films made an already fine film actor into a major British box-office star and no one seemed to notice that in the same year as

THE FIRST OF THE SOULFUL KILLERS: *THE BLUE LAMP* (1950).

the first of them, 1954, he also had made his first film for the exiled Joseph Losey, then on the run from the McCarthy tribunal and therefore unable even to use his own name as director. It was this film, *The Sleeping Tiger*, that pointed the way towards the future that Bogarde wanted to have in films, not *Doctor in the House*; but the success of the *Doctor* films was to thwart his chosen direction for at least another ten years.

'We made the film,' recalled Losey, 'not easily and not pleasantly: I worked anonymously without knowledge of British idiosyncrasies and with little confidence excepting what Dirk gave me. Insofar as he understood any of my political opinions he certainly didn't agree with them, so it took much courage and much

BELOW: WITH PRODUCER BETTY BOX, DIRECTOR RALPH THOMAS AND CO-STAR MICHAEL CRAIG ON LOCATION IN CANADA FOR *CAMPBELL'S KINGDOM* (1957). RIGHT: TRYING TO LOOK BOTH POETIC AND SEXY AS PER RANK ORGANISATION REQUIREMENTS.

acceptance to perform the unselfish act of faith which he did. Out of it grew a profound friendship and love which has endured much testing and some provocation.'

In a way Bogarde's enthusiasm to work with him at the moment of Losey's humiliation and Bogarde's fame gave Losey back his self-respect and his professional pride. And Losey honed Bogarde's already awesome natural talent into a technical marvel: a film actor capable of thinking his way into any role and giving it substance and dignity. Losey's admiration for Bogarde was entirely reciprocal. They were to make four more films together, each in its way a landmark of the British cinema. The words that now best describe his work — sensitivity, integrity, subtlety, courage — were earned at Losey's knee.

In 1961 this courage was needed for Dirk's decision to make *Victim*. On the surface this was a blackmail thriller. In fact, it was the first mainstream British film to treat homosexuality seriously and to suggest that husbands, fathers and productive members of the upper classes could also be gay. Dirk risked his immense popularity with a mainly female audience to play the barrister with a homosexual past, and was rewarded with the best reviews of his career so far. The *Evening News* raved, 'Today we must salute Dirk Bogarde. Applaud him for his courage and for the revelation of previously unplumbed depths of his talent.' And the *Evening Standard* said, 'Dirk Bogarde has a role that shows not only what a brilliant actor he is, but what a

courageous one he is too ... I predict that his brave, sensitive picture of an unhappy, terribly bewildered man will win him and this film a far wider audience.'

Wider still was the audience for *The Servant*, the film that brought him back to Joe Losey in 1963. Written by Harold Pinter and based on Robin Maugham's novel, this story of the manservant turning on his master revitalized Bogarde's career (by winning him the British

WITH JOE LOSEY AND TOM COURTENAY ON THE SET OF *KING AND COUNTRY* (1964).

WITH JULIE CHRISTIE IN JOHN
SCHLESINGER'S *DARLING*
(1965).

more British, institutions under their microscope the following year when they made *King and Country*, the story of the First World War Private Hamp (Tom Courtenay, in the role that confirmed his stardom) and his trial for desertion. As the defending counsel Bogarde awakened gradually to the injustice of the military system in a masterpiece of taut self-control, underplayed to prodigious effect. Not many major film-makers, or stars for that matter, were willing to take on the British sense of patriotism and show it for the jingoism it often is.

Bogarde's second BFA Best Actor award came from his performance as one of Julie Christie's many lovers in *Darling*, John Schlesinger's elegant satire on the Swinging Sixties. While other films of the time celebrated the freedoms and overturning of standards that came with the cult of the King's Road and Carnaby Street and the Beatles, Frederic Raphael's screenplay was already a morality tale about cocktails and laughter and what came after. Bogarde's essentially cool personality was perfect as a counterpoint to the heat of the subject matter.

But beyond that the prospects looked bleak for Bogarde's career. And then came Visconti and *Death in Venice*. He had worked with the great Italian director before, in *The Damned*, but the combination did not 'take'. With the barely

Film Academy's Best Actor award), and with it the whole concept of serious British film-making. As the roles reverse and the servant moves above stairs, the power games increase and the film examines both the class system and that particularly British clenched homosexuality in ever-darker cinematic performances, from Bogarde as the slimy cockney who is really in charge and from James Fox as the master who becomes the servant.

The same partnership put other, even

disguised portrait of Gustav Mahler in the character of Von Aschenbach, a composer and conductor come to Venice to remember and to die, they both found their masterpiece. The entire film is seen through the eyes of Bogarde's character: every moment is his experience, his obsessions, his memories, his life and his death, and this was the role for which all the others had been detailed rehearsals.

That year the Oscar for Best Actor was won by Gene Hackman, but it should have gone to Dirk Bogarde and everyone in the British film world, if not in Hollywood, knew it. Bogarde was not even nominated and remains to this day without an Oscar — one of the worst examples of the Academy's insularity and short-sightedness when it comes to handing out the statues. But statues were never what Dirk Bogarde was about. His films are about him, about acting, about subtlety and about art. And he came by it all honestly.

PUTTING ON THE HAT ...
PREPARING FOR HIS MASTERLY
ASCHENBACH ON THE VENICE
LIDO, 1971.

1 BORN TO ACT

'Childhood for me was basically a backyard, a spade and a bucket of mud with someone to look after you.'

Derek Jules Gaspard Ulric Niven van den Bogaerde had acting in his blood. Both his mother, the English actress Margaret Niven, and her father had been stage actors of some renown but it was visual rather than performing art that first attracted him, and that came from his father's side of the family. Conceived in Paris and born in a taxi in Hampstead on 28 March 1921, he was the elder son of Ulric van den Bogaerde and an actress just beginning to receive international recognition. With rotten timing, his mother's call to Hollywood came just three months after the wedding and Ulric made it clear that his new wife would have to choose between him and the movies. As Dirk was later to recall, 'The pact she made with my father lasted reasonably happily but the dull pain and the vague feeling of disappointment, even unachievement, was to remain buried away inside all of her life. And of course, all of ours.'

Ulric was Dutch but had already lived in England for many years. As Art Editor of *The Times*, Dirk's father was at the peak of his career and working such long hours that his son could never remember him home before nine. But his mother's preoccupation and his father's workload gave a small child time and opportunity to stretch his imagination. From the age of four he had been acting out his own plays for an audience of one, himself, in the privacy of his bedroom. This ability to focus on

DIRK'S FATHER, ULRIC VAN DEN BOGAERDE, AT HIS DESK AT *THE TIMES* IN 1938; HE WAS THE PAPER'S FIRST AND MOST INFLUENTIAL ART EDITOR.

himself was to stand him in good stead in later life as a film actor, when an inconvenient schedule made it impossible for his co-stars to be present for their joint scenes. 'I have done most of my best work to a white chalk mark because it's far better than doing it with an actor or an actress who is behind camera, ready to go home, really longing to get into that car, because they're not with you. They're just giving you the lines, usually with a cup of tea in one hand and a bun in the other. I've seen that happen. Reading the small adverts in the *Evening Standard* — seen that happen. So I say, "Leave it. Let them go. Give me a chalk mark." My best friend is a chalk mark.'

As described by Dirk in the first volume of his autobiography, it was an idyllic childhood. Interestingly, twenty years later he was acknowledging his mother's alcoholism and the effect of her problems on him and his sister Elizabeth and brother Gareth. 'She was in resentment all her life from which we suffered.'

Dirk's early life was divided into what his beloved nanny, Lally, explained to him as the inevitable change in seasons: 'You can't have a good summer without a really hard winter.' So the summers of Dirk's childhood were romantically started in a cottage in Sussex where a neighbour, Virginia Woolf, would hover around the garden offering bunches of flowers to the local fishermen.

A good-looking, fanciful child, who had inherited both his mother's theatricality and his father's talent for art, he made his very

first stage appearance as a schoolboy, in the local amateur dramatic society's production of *Alf's Button*. 'An inauspicious start to my career. Half naked, dressed in baggy chiffon knickers and a gold turban, I stood impassively, arms folded across my chest, holding a paper scimitar in one hand and my terror in the other. I never moved and no one really saw me but there is a picture of me in the local paper to prove it. I was cold, frightened, idiotic. But I had started and nothing now was ever going to stop me.'

Ulric and Margaret were considerate enough to supply Dirk and his younger sister, Elizabeth, with the requisite number of eccentric relatives, including two grandfathers, one of whom, a traveller and artist, had abandoned his family to live in some squalor in Brighton, while the other, an old actor, had been found guilty by his wife of some nameless crime and was forced to eke out his old age sitting by the kitchen fire, far away from any other members of his household.

But if the summers were long and golden on the South Downs and on family holidays in Normandy, winter came abruptly with the arrival, when Dirk was thirteen, of a younger brother, Gareth, who, much to Dirk and Elizabeth's horror, immediately became the centre of the household. Only then did Dirk discover that their cottage home had never belonged to the family after all and so there could be no return to that particular paradise. At this already vulnerable moment for Dirk, his father decided that the sooner he was trained in art the better, in the curious belief that his role at *The Times* was hereditary and could be passed on to his suitably qualified elder son. It is not clear why he thought that the best place to obtain those qualifications was north of the border, but he did, and Dirk was abruptly sent to Scotland to board with an uncle and aunt who lived in dismal poverty, and to attend a wildly unsuitable local technical college, Allan Glen's School in Glasgow.

The experience was nothing short of disastrous. Dirk was mercilessly taunted at school for his southern accent and apparent grandeur, a sin for which the punishment was to have his head stuffed down a lavatory pan. Life was not much improved when a local pervert took him home for tea, insisted that the boy should disguise himself as Boris Karloff playing a mummy, leaving only his genitals exposed to fulfil his host's eccentric fantasy. Not surprisingly, Dirk has never returned to Glasgow.

He managed to get himself back into the family fold in London by the time he was fifteen, but only on his father's condition that, following the completion of his general education at University College School, he would attend the Chelsea Polytechnic (now the Chelsea College of Art), where he took a course in commercial art with an emphasis on stage and film design.

His principal teachers there were Henry Moore and Graham Sutherland. Moore's best gift to Dirk was the art of perspective, though Sutherland failed totally to teach him the elements of painting the human body. 'Which is why, to this day, I can still do a remarkably good bird's-eye view of the Piazza San Marco, Times Square, or even Kennington Oval, looking as if they had been struck by bubonic plague. My perspectives are empty; however, I am really good at people leaning out of windows.' Bogarde is being characteristically self-deprecatory here, for some of his later wartime drawings are held in museum collections and his more than competent pen and ink sketches highlight his own published memoirs.

By now in his late teens, he was under considerable pressure from his father to

DIRK WITH THE DIRECTOR BASIL DEARDEN IN 1963. DEARDEN GAVE DIRK HIS FIRST REALLY DRAMATIC ROLE, IN *THE BLUE LAMP* (1950), AND WENT ON TO WORK WITH HIM ON *THE GENTLE GUNMAN* (1952) AND *VICTIM* (1961).

persevere with his art training and he did try. But there was now another influence on his life. The more Dirk's father tried to urge him towards a life in art, sending him on to study colour photogravure at Sun Engraving, the more Dirk began to think about the other great line of his heritage, the theatre, to which his mother and grandfather had both belonged.

It was, of course, a strong connection, so it didn't take Dirk long to find, among the Chelsea art students, those who were already painting backdrops for amateur theatricals and before long, having worn his father down in a long war of attrition, Dirk began to involve himself with the theatre. His father's opposition was a source of pain to him because it was always him that he wanted to please and, right up until Ulric's death in 1973, it was his advice and approval that Dirk sought on every aspect of his career. 'He didn't want me to be an actor,' Dirk said, 'but I consulted him on everything because I loved him very much.' In a way Ulric had already lost the battle. One of Dirk's godparents was the actress Yvonne Arnaud, and one of the few bright points of his Glasgow sojourn was being allowed, at the age of thirteen, to join her on stage in Glasgow for a courtroom drama. He was hooked.

At first he found himself drawn into the amateur theatre, where he was originally billed by mistake as 'Birk Gocart', an error which proved too expensive to correct on his earliest poster. As early as 1939 he turns up for his very first film appearance as an extra in a crowd scene of a George Formby

comedy, *Come On, George*. Still trying to fulfil Ulric's dream, Dirk took on what turned out to be a miserable but short apprenticeship in printing. But, at the age of nineteen, in 1940, in the first year of the Second World War, he suddenly found himself painting scenery for peanuts, appearing fleetingly on stage and even getting briefly engaged to Annie Deans, a young actress, in what he was to recall as the panic of youth and wartime.

It was at the Q Theatre, by Kew Bridge, that he made his professional debut, in 1939, but only because one of the cast of J. B. Priestley's *When We Are Married* fell ill; his official job at Q had been as assistant to the set designer, call boy, tea-maker, glue-boiler (wigs and false beards were then held on with a noxious substance that had to be boiled then cooled before it could be applied) and general dogsbody. The director of *When We Are Married* was Basil Dearden, who later directed Dirk in two of the best British films of the 1960s: *Victim* and *The Mind Benders*. But in 1939 Dearden was less than impressed with his new acting recruit, whose only line was: 'My Lord, the carriage awaits without,' commenting wryly, 'Oh Christ, I know there's a war on now, they're rationing the talent.' Dearden and Bogarde would be lifelong friends from then on.

Q was the breakthrough, for only a few months later he had made it to the West End, repeating a role he had first taken on there as the office boy in another Priestley drama, *Cornelius*. Air-raid sirens interrupted the first night but *The Times* noted proudly that 'nobody left the theatre', and Dirk, billed now as Derek Bogaerde, achieved his first review when *The Stage* noted, 'He is a sulky true-to-life office boy.' But that was only part of the story. The other part was the sheer excitement of going on stage. 'The noise of that curtain going up, and the audience and the house lights going down and the audience voice, because it becomes one voice, softening away to nothing and the curtain going up and the wooosssshhhh. You can hear it on the stage, you can't hear it in the audience; it is, I suppose, a prelude to "You're on!" and your heart races and the adrenalin flows and you're on, and that's it and you're there to entertain for two and a half hours or whatever it is and it is one of the most exciting noises in the world.'

A few weeks later the Blitz succeeded, where the London theatregoers would not, in closing down all evening theatre performances. But he had found his life's work. For better or worse, Dirk Bogarde was now an actor. In a way, of course, he always had been.

He was engaged for the season at the Amersham Rep and it was there that he was discovered by Anthony Forwood. Not that Forwood's first impression was all that favourable: going backstage, he told Dirk,

WITH JENNY LAIRD IN DIRK'S WEST END DÉBUT AS THE 'SULKY BUT TRUE-TO-LIFE' OFFICE BOY IN J.B. PRIESTLEY'S *CORNELIUS* (WESTMINSTER THEATRE, 1940).

'You were perfectly frightful but you have a quality. I don't know what it is, but we might put it to some use.' Starting from when they met again after the war, Forwood, who presumably had worked out in the intervening years what that quality was, would take care of him for the next fifty years. Until his death in 1988, of the deadly combination of Parkinson's disease and cancer, he was agent, friend, business manager and, following the breakdown of his marriage to Glynis Johns, life partner. 'Tony found me at eighteen and we were together for fifty years, except during the war and his marriage; people thought my calling him "Forwood" in all my books made him sound like the gardener but he was always "Forwood" to me. People are far too obsessed nowadays with homosexuality.

Ours was a totally platonic relationship; Tony was a rather puritanical figure who happened to hate the idea of homosexuality.'

THE HOUSE HE MOST LOVED: DIRK IN 1974 AT LE HAUT CLERMONT, THE FARMHOUSE OUTSIDE GRASSE IN THE SOUTH OF FRANCE WHICH HE SHARED FOR TWENTY YEARS WITH TONY FORWOOD.

A slightly military figure of great discipline and organizational skills, Forwood was to give up all his other clients to chart Dirk's steadily rising star, as he allowed Dirk's postwar career to take over his entire professional life. Selflessly he guided, managed and prodded Dirk, while handling all contracts, whether from Hollywood moguls or for the plumber's work in the house they shared for many years outside Grasse in the South of France. After his death Dirk admitted that he had never written a cheque nor even seen a bank statement.

Forwood's first contribution to Dirk's career was decidedly eccentric. With many London shows, including *Cornelius*, closed by the Blitz, a Herbert Farjeon revue called *Diversion* was surviving for matinées at Wyndhams with an amazing cast led by Edith Evans, Bernard Miles, Joyce Grenfell, Peter Ustinov and Dorothy Dickson. Dirk was pitched briefly into their midst for his only ever appearance as a song-and-dance man. He was only nineteen and already he knew that his future did not lie in musicals.

From there he was conscripted by ENSA – the Entertainments National Service Association, irreverently known as Every Night Something Awful – to play in a terrible tour of Arnold Ridley's *The Ghost Train*. This was such a miserable experience that even the call-up papers which summoned him to Catterick army camp and the Second World War came as something of a relief. He wasn't afraid; like all young men at the beginning of the war, he knew himself to be immortal.

'My wartime name was Pip: there was no pixie-like reason for this ... maddened by my calm, bovine, agreeable incomprehension of anything remotely connected to the business of my becoming a signaller, my exhausted Catterick instructor suddenly hurled his piece of chalk, the book of instructions, a duster, and finally his cap at me and roared for quick delivery from my dumb bewilderment, 'You bloody give me the pip!'

So Pip he became and Pip he remained until his demob. During the time he was Pip his realization not just of his own mortality but also of the darkness in men's souls stayed with him long after he became Dirk again, and that realization can be seen

sometimes in his best performances. While he was Pip he also found out what friendship is — that close, trusting partnership between people who must depend on each other for their very lives — and he has written touchingly in his offhand literary style about his best wartime friend, Chris.

Dirk's war is best chronicled in two of his own autobiographies, *Snakes and Ladders* (1978) and *Cleared for Takeoff* (1995), and what is interesting is how the mood of his memory has changed in those seventeen years. *Snakes and Ladders* offers a reasonably upbeat diary of long months of inactivity at Catterick, followed by the

IN 1944, ATTACHED TO THE ARMY INTELLIGENCE PHOTOGRAPHIC UNIT IN THE RUN-UP TO D-DAY.

crossing of the Rhine and eventual action in the Far East. It's not until *Cleared for Takeoff* that he can bring himself to describe in close-up the sheer bloody terrors of close combat.

Throughout the war he wrote compulsively to Ulric, trying, as he says, to outdo Wilfred Owen, the great First World War poet, and Ulric wrote once a week, always signing his letters with the phrase that kept Dirk going: 'All love, Pa.' Margaret never wrote at all, occasionally adding a line to the bottom of Ulric's letters: 'Pa will have given you all the news. Love, Ma'; and it was to his father alone that Dirk poured out the misery of those days and nights. Ulric was later to take a rather odd credit for Dirk's survival of the war when accused by his son of having inflicted his lifelong claustrophobia on him. It was caused, Dirk said, by Ulric's insistence on regularly shutting him up in a drawer as an infant so that the baby's crying didn't disturb his workaholic father's sleep. Well, said Ulric, the drawer had plenty of ventilation, and anyway it gave Dirk a taste for the open air which saved him from wartime death in bombed-out buildings.

Dirk's temperament is, despite his exotic and foreign forebears, very English and held in, so he seemed in the earlier book to be trying to dismiss the entire Second World War as little more than an inconvenient disruption to his career, full of amusing anecdotes and witty accounts of discomfort. It is not therefore surprising that his war was rarely discussed by him and only

glimpsed in his subsequent film performances. His demonstrable lack of talent for the Signal Corps did not dissuade the Army from finding a way to use his obvious expertise and visual training. He rose to the rank of major in Intelligence, specializing in the analysis of aerial photographs. His job was to read enemy emplacements from photographic intelligence reports and, even during the liberation of Belgium, he was shocked to discover from his photographs that a Panzer division was just the other side of the town from which the Allied troops were embarking.

Throughout the war he and his friend Chris, also a trained draughtsman, who was to become a successful commercial artist in civvy street, occupied the many idle and cold and waiting moments by creating their own impressions of the misery of war. These are among the most vivid evocations of his army life, and shortly after demob he and Chris had a joint exhibition of their war paintings, which they attended in worn uniforms and modest medals, and sold all of them. Some are now in the collection of the Imperial War Museum.

He was demobbed from Singapore but he had been in all the major European and Far Eastern theatres of war, recalling in later memoirs the horrors of enemy attack and the black humour of the battlefields. One of Ulric's last pre-war instructions to his wayward son was, 'Observe, notice, compare, and keep silent,' and it was precisely that admonition which was to colour both his acting and his writing in the

future. Who else but a son capable of following those parental orders could write that his first experience of sleeping with a whore in wartime Cyprus was 'about as stimulating as watching tin rust'?

The wartime atrocities he had witnessed, the devastation of a land-mine explosion at which he could not bring himself to shoot a fatally maimed soldier, and the indescribable privations of the Bergen-Belsen concentration camp that he had witnessed as part of the liberation forces ('I realized that I was looking at Dante's Inferno') literally shocked him into silence. 'We never spoke of it again to anyone.'

In Calcutta, the sight of a British officer beating an Indian with a stick brought home for the first time the horrors of racism, but again the reality was too much emotional baggage to examine and he consigns it to his private nightmares, as if just being present at the event includes him in the guilt. He later pretended to Joseph Losey that none of this had happened, that he had sailed through virtually unscathed. 'I had a lovely war, Aide to the General. Very giddy and dapper. Arranging dinner parties,'

was how he fantasized it. The reality was much darker. In later life he has always given the impression of an intelligence beyond that of the characters he plays and a burden that is too heavy for description.

The Pip who disembarked from the *Monarch of Bermuda* in Liverpool was not the Pip who had regarded his call-up with resignation mixed with a small measure of excitement. This Pip, like so many young men of his generation, had seen too much. This Pip left the transportation ship in Liverpool and set out for Haywards Heath in his pork-pie hat and his speckled cotton and wool suit. But it was Dirk who arrived there.

ON ACTIVE SERVICE HE ALSO FOUND TIME TO WORK AS AN UNOFFICIAL WAR ARTIST: THIS 'VIEW FROM MY TENT' IS NOW IN THE BRITISH MUSEUM COLLECTION.

2 FIRST STEPS

'*Within a year I had a mistress, a house in London and a seven-year contract with J. Arthur Rank.*'

Demobilization came to Dirk as something of a shock; whatever the horrors of his war he had actually relished five years of never having to make a major decision about his personal life or future career. The Army gave you orders and you followed them. Now, suddenly, there were no orders and even worse than the demob suit and the appalling pork-pie hat which the Army graciously provided, there was a sharp letter from the War Office accounts department noting that he had inadvertently been overpaid by £800 since 1939 and could he please refund the money as soon as possible? Quite how he was to do this the Army didn't explain and it seemed unlikely even to Dirk that a brief pre-war career in a Farjeon revue and a transfer from Q had left such an indelible impression on producers, directors or agents as to guarantee immediate postwar employment in the theatre, particularly employment lucrative enough to assure the War Office that he could meet his enormous debt. His new life was also overshadowed by a car crash. '[On] VJ night in 1945 I drove a jeep into a line of men — British Army deserters — on a road outside Calcutta. I had wretchedly killed two people in monsoon rain.' Although he was completely exonerated of all blame and grand cars were later to become part of his star image, from that night Dirk never drove again.

And it was not as though he was the only actor returning from the war in debt and in vague hopes of picking up his nascent career; he wasn't even especially sure that he wanted to. However, the absence of any other opportunity, and the certainty that he was not cut out to be a commercial artist, led him on the

OPPOSITE: DIRK'S SECOND FILM, *ESTHER WATERS* (1948), WAS THE ONE IN WHICH HE PLAYED A GAMBLING FOOTMAN TURNED BOOKMAKER AND SEDUCER OF ESTHER: THE ROLE CAME TO HIM ONLY AFTER IT HAD BEEN REJECTED BY STEWART GRANGER.

STUDIO PORTRAITS FROM DIRK'S
EARLY RANK YEARS, AS HE MADE
THE GRADUAL TRANSITION FROM
TEENAGE IDOL TO MATURE
LEADING MAN.

body. Later on he was to realize that his face had two distinct aspects: the left side was more even, with a larger earlobe balancing the nose, the right was lobeless, more angular – just the thing for menace when he needed it. In 1970 he told Ann Guerin, 'Every set was built for my left profile, nobody ever saw the right side of my face in something like thirty pictures. I was the Loretta Young of England.' Not everyone saw his potential, at least not at first. Even the Rank Organisation, for whom he was to be the biggest money-spinner for fourteen years, initially told him that with a neck too thin, a head too small and one leg slightly shorter than the other, he really should think about some other career. At this time, in any case, his heart was still loosely attached to the theatre, though he was in such despair about ever getting another job in it that he had begun to think seriously about becoming an English teacher at a prep school.

Neither his old friends at the Q Theatre nor Peter Ustinov, by this time an established star, held out much hope until, at a random audition — Dirk had come to

long and forlorn round of agents' offices, where he spent much of 1946.

All he had to sell was his undoubted intelligence and, more significantly, his looks. He had, after all, no formal training as an actor and very little experience. But he was beautiful. Bogarde has never had to watch his weight and remains today the slim, elegant figure he was in those early auditions. He had inherited from Margaret an even, oval face and large, dark eyes fringed with long lashes. The vulnerability in those eyes was offset by the strength in the chin and the proportions of the slim read for a part in a BBC television script and had stumbled accidentally into the wrong studio — the director, Allan Davis, was casting a new play for the Actors Reunion Theatre and decided that Dirk was just the man he was looking for. The role was that of a modern-dress Jesus Christ and it played mornings only for the benefit of any agents or talent scouts eager enough to increase their client list.

Thus it was, with a little biblical help, that Dirk got himself an agent, Freddy Joachim, who first of all sorted out his name, losing all its foreign spellings, and more usefully, got him into one of the very first live BBC Television dramas, a production of *Rope* which gave Dirk the satisfaction of seeing for the first time his name above the title even if only in the *Radio Times*. He played a student who commits a murder for fun. It was based on the famous American case of Leopold and Loeb, two college boys involved in a homosexual affair.

From the very beginning of his career this raised questions about Dirk's own sexuality, as, later, did his work in such movies as *Victim*, *The Servant* and *Death in Venice*. Either he was the hearty, larky, randy Dr Simon Sparrow of his juvenile lead years at Rank or a vastly more intriguing figure, suppressing a whole other life until it found a voice in some of his best roles. At the time of *Death in Venice* (1971) one or two critics, notably in America, felt that this had to be the triumph of a gay actor. While Dirk never sued, he carefully denied the suggestion whenever possible.

'People can't understand how you can be unmarried, have an adoring family and simply wish to be on your own. I am not a homosexual, but if that's what people want to think, they'll think it. The truth is, I dread possession. No one is ever allowed to come too close and the limit is always fixed by myself. So far and no further.'

Years later he told the interviewer Russell Harty, 'I'm still in the shell, and you're not going to crack it, ducky.' All through his career he had chosen to be particularly circumspect about his private life. What today seems an extraordinary achievement, greater even than stardom over the next forty years, must surely be his absolute privacy in this

area, all the more remarkable given that he has published seven volumes of autobiography. In those, he has written at length about at least three affairs with women; he has never once commented on the suggestion that his interest in homosexuality was anything other than artistic and compassionate, except to characterize his forty-year life with Tony Forwood as asexual, often adding the intriguing piece of information that Forwood was anti-homosexual.

Dirk has always said that their life

together was a deep friendship and the house-sharing of two increasingly confirmed bachelors. 'Homosexuality,' he once noted, 'is now rearing its head a great deal. I find it both tiresome and boring. There was such a thing as your "mate", your "best friend", a close relationship that a woman could not possibly share. That's not homosexuality — look at any football team.' If ever they get around, in the fullness of time, to opening that particular closet, it could still be that all they will ever find there are Dirk's old gardening clothes.

In his first starring role, then, Dirk was playing a complicated, tortured but highly sexually charged character and it was a forerunner of so many of his future roles. Yet he himself had

WITH KENNETH MORE IN THE 1947 STAGE VERSION OF *POWER WITHOUT GLORY*. THE TEAM THAT WAS TO REUNITE FOR THE EARLY *DOCTOR* MOVIES WAS HERE INVOLVED IN A MURDER PLOT.

no hope that it would lead to anything else. After the live transmission, Dirk reluctantly went back to the anonymous round of auditions. And a few months later, in February 1947, one of them yielded the role that would make his name. In fact, he went to audition for a television play he had been sent and mistook the studio. He waited two hours to be seen by the producer until the commissionaire kindly told him that the BBC people had left. As he rose to totter disconsolately out of the building, a breathless woman accosted him on the stairs, shouting that they had been waiting for him to audition for a theatre play and where had he been? He didn't tell them he was not who they had been waiting for until after he had read for them and been engaged to play the role. As he left he dropped the redundant television script into the nearest wastepaper basket. 'When I threw away that BBC script I didn't realize I was getting rid of my anonymity for the rest of my life. It simply never occurred to me.'

The play, first staged at the little New Lindsay Theatre, was Michael Clayton-Hutton's *Power without Glory*, a tense thriller about the impact of a murder on an ordinary working-class family in South London. In its cast were not only Dirk, who, as the murderer, had the flashiest part, but also Kenneth More, Dandy Nichols and Maureen Pryor. All

were to go on to stardom but were, at the time, totally unknown. It was Dirk who was the first to be noticed by those who could do his career the most good and who would make him a star. He certainly made the greatest on-stage impression on the producer, Peter Daubeny, who would later recall, 'Suddenly, there rushed onto the stage a breathless figure, half choking with emotion: a slight, dark youth, radiating a curious, almost hypnotic power: every movement, every inflection of his voice, uncannily suggested the poetry of the gutter, of a lost soul. Beyond any doubt, here was an actor of the first rank.'

An early distinguished visitor to the tiny theatre in Notting Hill was Noël Coward, so impressed that he wanted to move virtually the whole cast into his new drama, *Peace in Our Time*, about an imaginary 1940 invasion of Britain by the Germans. On his visit backstage, Noël had given Dirk his usual finger-wagging rebuke, 'Never, ever take a pill before the show. Never take a drink until after curtainfall, and above all, never ever go into the cinema.' But during the run of *Power without Glory*, Dirk had got his first adult role in a movie, *Dancing with Crime*. Although he only had one line to say — 'Calling Car 2345, calling Car 2345'— he was on his way. For that one day's work he earned £20, twice what he was getting for a week at the New Lindsay. So when the tiny Wessex Film company offered him a contract for a movie called *Esther Waters* Dirk decided to ignore Noël's advice and sign it.

Noël was appalled. Summoning Dirk to

his flat in Gerald Road, Belgravia, he was reassuring as he turned on the light in the hall. 'Go straight ahead, there's the front door, and by the way I shan't jump on you. I'm not the type and Gerald Road Police Station is immediately opposite you. Would you care for a whistle or will you merely shout?' Humour aside, Coward spent that whole evening trying to make Dirk change his mind about the movies, but to no avail. 'I think you are being a cunt,' was his parting shot as his dream of Dirk in *Peace in Our Time* disappeared. Despite this pithy dismissal, they were

IN *ESTHER WATERS* WITH KATHLEEN RYAN – 'AS GOOD PLAYING THE UNHAPPY GIRL AS IS DIRK AS THE MAN WHO DESTROYS HER: BOTH NEWCOMERS ARE WORTH WATCHING' (*DAILY MIRROR*).

to remain friends until Noël's death.

Between his signing by Wessex Films, whose distributors were the giant Hollywood-leaning J. Arthur Rank, and its production, Dirk was signed by Rank to a seven-year contract. They immediately started getting their money's worth for the £30 a week they were paying him but didn't give the inexperienced film star much guidance. 'I walked around with hundreds of pounds' worth of costumes on my back in a daze. When I asked the director how I should play a scene he told me, "You're the actor, you should know."' In fact Dirk didn't, but at least *Esther Waters* began his education in film. Set in the 1880s, it was the story of a maid (played by Kathleen Ryan) who is made pregnant by a footman. She ends up in the workhouse while he dies, ruined by his gambling debts.

The reviews were patchy but the *Sunday Express* at least thought 'Dirk Bogarde, another newcomer, justifies his quick jump to stardom'. On the other hand, the *Star* considered Bogarde 'not experienced enough to avoid being overwhelmed by the encircling gloom', while the *News Chronicle* found him 'likeable and feckless, but entirely lacking in authority'. Both of these two less flattering reviews accorded precisely with his own view of his first shot at movie acting. 'By the time *Esther Waters*

WITH KATHLEEN RYAN (RIGHT) AS THE HOUSEMAID AND LALAGE LEWIS AS THE NIECE OF HIS WEALTHY EMPLOYER.

was released, I had already made two other films. Otherwise I wouldn't ever have worked again.'

It was only midway through the shooting that Dirk discovered that his doubts were entirely justified: the role had originally been offered to Stewart Granger and it was Granger's last-minute refusal that catapulted Dirk into a starring role. Dirk was pretty tense by now, so he took his father's criticism seriously when Ulric, on seeing a poster for *Esther Waters* in the London Underground, accused him of bringing the family name into disrepute. Much later Ulric confirmed that he had been joking, but Dirk was terribly upset for a long time.

Power without Glory had by this time transferred to the West End, where its run was more of a convulsive two-month stagger, confirming Dirk's view that he might do better in the movies. Just before *Esther Waters* started shooting, the London representative of a Hollywood studio decided that they too might be interested in him, but not as Dirk Bogarde.

Their plan was that he should go to live in Mexico for two years, learn Spanish and then slip into Hollywood, where he would suddenly and miraculously be discovered as the great new Latin lover, Riccardo something, and put straight into a remake of *Blood and Sand*, playing the role comfortably occupied previously by Rudolph Valentino (1922) and later by Tyrone Power (1941). To sweeten the deal, the earnest lady from LaLaland offered him a bungalow in Pacific Palisades, and — most important this, in the status-conscious movie capital — a foreign car (provided it was nothing grander than a Volkswagen Beetle). But what finally turned Dirk off the deal was the list she handed him of what she described as 'nice clean girls' who were under contract to

WITH KATHLEEN RYAN IN
ESTHER WATERS.

the studio, one of whom he would be
required to marry during his first
year in California although he would
be allowed to get divorced a year
later. The studio, she assured him,
would handle all the 'details'.

Dirk fled, vowing to avoid
Hollywood at all costs. 'I thought,
I'm twenty-six, I've just finished a
war with seven medals. What am I
doing with these people? I tore up
the contract and walked home in the
snow.' Besides, there was another
very good reason for staying at
home. A magazine called *The Sketch*
listed the four young men most likely
in their view to achieve success. Of
the four, one was Dirk's producer,
Peter (later Sir Peter) Daubeny, one
disappeared without trace, one was
Dirk and the other was Harold
Wilson.

With the Rank salary, Dirk was
now financially secure, if not flush.
He could afford his own home and
for the first time his taste for luxury and
space asserted itself. He rented a house, an
enormous but shabby five-storey job in
Belgravia's Chester Row. It cost £10 a week,
nearly a third of what Rank was paying
him, but it was worth it. He needed
someone to look after it and him and he
invited Nan Baildon to move in. He had
met her in Calcutta during the war, when
she was a squadron leader in the WAAF.
They had travelled together through the Far
East and, although she was about ten years
older, he was tremendously fond of her.

Life in Chester Row was fun. They
bought a table at Peter Jones and started to
give parties. Dirk didn't realize that Pimms,
the tipple of choice among his friends, was
alcoholic, so he used to lace it with lashings
of gin, an unaccustomed luxury he could
now sometimes afford. Tales of his generous
hospitality spread. Soon he was stumbling
over their friends in the morning on his way
to Pinewood Studios, asleep where they had
fallen on his carpet. Nan moderated the
Pimms, but they enjoyed themselves hugely,
while Dirk set about building a star career.

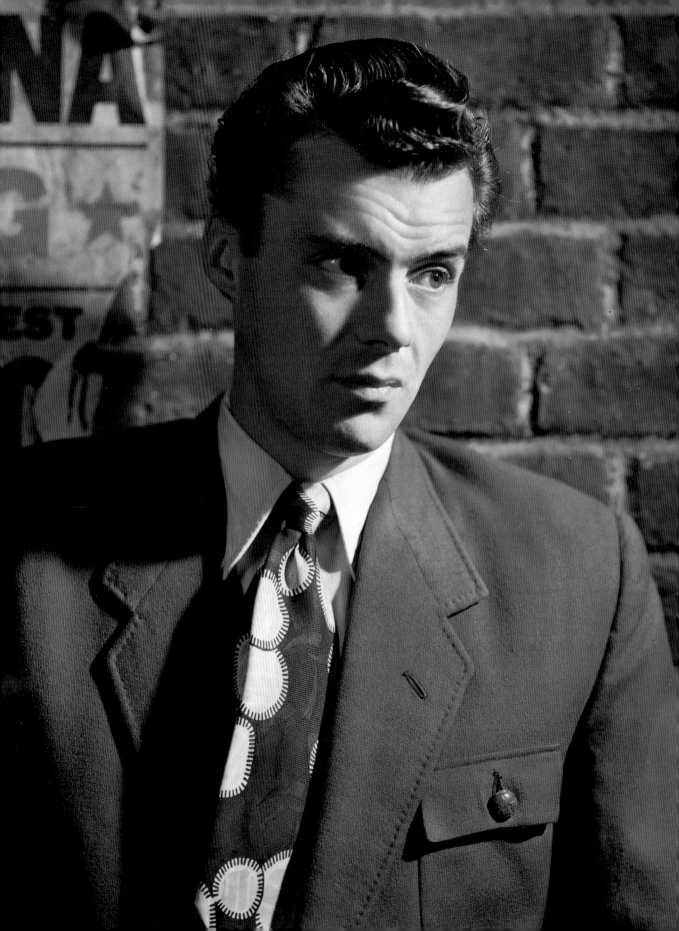

3 SHIFTING GEAR

'First there was the war and then the peace to cope with, and then suddenly I was a film star. It all happened too soon.'

In the years that followed, Rank kept Dirk moving from picture to picture. After *Esther Waters* came *The Alien Corn*, part of a collection of Somerset Maugham short stories released as *Quartet*. Dirk played the young, poetic aristocrat who passionately wants to be a concert pianist until Françoise Rosay breaks it to him that he has no chance whatsoever of success, whereupon he takes his own life. In those early days Dirk seemed to specialize in tragic end-of-picture deaths.

He found himself slung into a speedway-racing action picture called *Once a Jolly Swagman*. It would be hard to think of anybody, even on the then current Rank roster, who was less suited to such a tale. Dirk's terror of all machinery meant that his performance as the champ who tries to organize the other riders into a militant trade union was less than wholly convincing and Dirk was not reassured when the director, Jack Lee, told him that his performance might be improved if he would take his motorbike home every night, stand it in his bedroom and 'love it like a woman'.

J. Arthur Rank were determined to get full value from the £50 a week they were now paying their latest contract artist and in 1948 Dirk worked all the time, going straight from *Swagman* (which was chiefly remarkable for being the first time he got mobbed by girls waiting outside the studio for autographs) to two more forgettable movies. There was *Dear Mr Prohack*, in which he played the son of a

AS THE ULTIMATELY SUICIDAL PIANIST IN SOMERSET MAUGHAM'S *THE ALIEN CORN*, HERE WITH HONOR BLACKMAN IN ONE OF THE SHORT STORIES THAT MADE UP *QUARTET* (1948).

ABOVE: *ONCE A JOLLY
SWAGMAN* (1948): AMONG THE
FANS WHO WERE TO PUT AN
ABRUPT END TO HIS STAGE
CAREER.

RIGHT: WITH GLYNIS JOHNS IN
DEAR MR PROHACK (1949), AN
ADAPTATION OF THE ARNOLD
BENNETT NOVEL ABOUT A
FAMILY AND A FORTUNE.

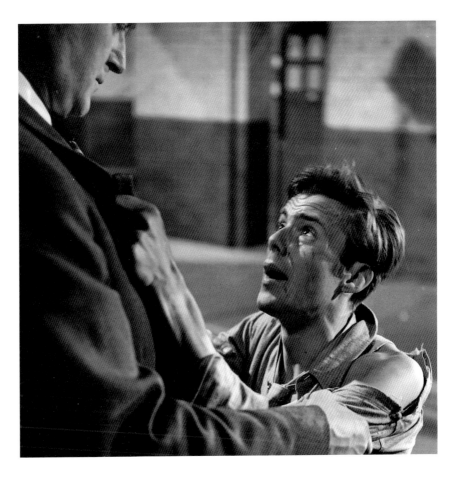

businessman who suddenly comes into a private fortune ('Dirk Bogarde is a boy with possibilities,' *Daily Mirror*; 'Mr Bogarde is adequate as the son,' *Daily Graphic*) and then *Boys in Brown*, where he was one of a gang of Borstal boys organizing a breakout.

Even in such a year as this, Dirk found the time to get back to the stage at his beloved Q Theatre for two more plays. *For Better for Worse*, which he was to film six years later, was a cosy comedy about newlyweds sharing a small flat. *Sleep on My Shoulder* was a more ambitious, although not wholly successful, fantasy about a group of wartime survivors (Dirk was a blind RAF pilot) coming together in a bombed Chelsea pub to discuss what their lives might otherwise have been.

By the end of 1949 things at Rank were looking up too: he was shooting *The Blue Lamp*, where he played a young thug who killed lovable Jack Warner as Sergeant Dixon, only to see him reincarnated some

AS THE BORSTAL BOY WITH JACK WARNER AS THE PRISON GOVERNOR IN *BOYS IN BROWN* (1949), ONE OF THE EARLY POSTWAR 'REALISM' FILMS ABOUT PRISON LIFE.

IN *SLEEP ON MY SHOULDER*
(1949), ONE OF HIS NOW
INCREASINGLY RARE STAGE
APPEARANCES, HE PLAYED AN
EX-RAF PILOT BLINDED IN THE
WAR. FAITH BROOK WAS HIS
GIRLFRIEND.

time later as the lead in
one of the longest-running
of all BBC television
series. During the shoot of
The Blue Lamp Dirk told
Picturegoer, 'Everyone
used to tell me not to act in front of a
camera. Don't move a muscle of your face,
make no big gestures, keep your voice low,
and above all, remember that you are not in
a theatre. And poor old Bogarde believed
them. I went up into the world of stars like
a damp rocket and fell silently to earth in a
flurry of sparks. Of course, you have to act
in front of a camera. It's quite different
acting from the stage but you simply must
act ... when we started work on *The Blue
Lamp* the director Basil Dearden [one of
Bogarde's original supporters] said to me,
"Act as if you were on the stage. I'll stop
you if you go too far," and so I did.'

The Blue Lamp was also notable for

being the first of the semi-documentary
police adventures which were later to
spread from the cinema to television as one
of the most consistently popular formats.
This one might almost have been a
recruiting picture for Scotland Yard, which
was as delighted with the number of new
applicants for the beat as was J. Arthur
Rank with his box-office takings. In his first
starring villain role as the boy gangster,
Dirk managed to suggest the sexiness of
evil, forever fondling his gun as though it
were growing out of him and suggesting a
strong link between sexuality and murder.
This was perhaps the first British example
of the street-smart violent but sexy criminal
already on view in Hollywood in films such
as *The Naked City*.

The day after the film was released,
Bogarde telephoned Earl St John, the Rank
chief who was to remain implacably
opposed to his work for all of twenty years,
to gloat over the reviews. 'Unfortunately,'
replied St John, 'we have no more roles for
mixed-up delinquents just at the moment.'
But Dirk got the last laugh. *The Blue Lamp*
was the most successful British film of the
entire year.

All this didn't allow much time for
domestic bliss and back home in Chester
Row the relationship with Nan was
becoming tense. Nan was, after all, in her
mid-thirties and her biological clock was
ticking. There was no room in Dirk's single-
minded and inexorable rise for a family.
Something had to give and that something
was Nan. On New Year's Day 1950, at the
start of a new decade, as they tidied up the

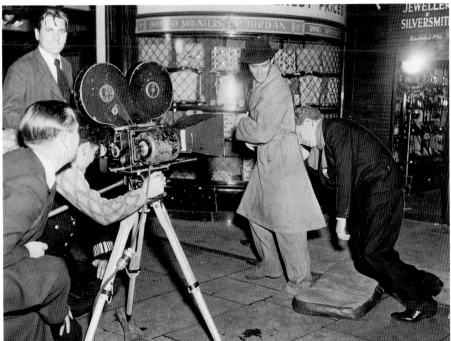

ABOVE: WITH PEGGY EVANS –
AND AN ALREADY ALMOST
SEXUAL FONDNESS FOR THE GUN
WITH WHICH HE WAS TO KILL
SERGEANT DIXON – IN *THE BLUE
LAMP*.

LEFT: SHOOTING THE SHOOTER
IN *THE BLUE LAMP*: NOTE THE
CUSHION ON WHICH ONE OF HIS
ENEMIES IS TO FALL.

41

house after the previous evening's party the frustration spilled over into a furious row and Nan retreated in tears.

Dirk, as always, went to Ulric for advice and was told that unless he could honestly say he was in love with Nan, he had no business even thinking about marrying her. He couldn't. In Dirk's much later recollection Ulric was unrelenting. He insisted that the act of a gentleman in that situation was to set Nan free. The only honourable course would be for Dirk to tell Nan that they had no future. And, Ulric continued, the demands of Dirk's profession made it impossible for him to be the kind of devoted husband Nan needed.

JUST THREE LITTLE CONTRACT BOYS AT THE RANKERY: DIRK IN CLOSE IF UNLIKELY HARMONY WITH GUY ROLFE AND DEREK BOND IN 1949.

'Cut her free,' he told his son unequivocally. He didn't. The relationship limped on for another year but it was effectively over and when she left Nan took with her the cat and the last vestiges of Dirk's war. She was the last person who ever called him Pip. And ever afterwards Dirk saw himself as 'the wrecker'.

Back in the boardroom of J. Arthur Rank, they had still, in spite of *The Blue Lamp*, formed no particular attachment to Dirk and no real idea of the kind of work he should be doing. Accordingly, he was loaned out to Gainsborough Pictures for a costume thriller. *So Long at the Fair* is the famous story of the man who disappears without trace at the Paris Great Exhibition of 1889. Dirk played a young artist who comes to the aid of the missing man's sister (Jean Simmons) in a tale of Kafkaesque horror in which nothing is quite what it seems. Most importantly for Dirk, at the age of twenty-nine, this was a film to prove that his talents need not always walk on the shadowy, seedier side of the Soho streets.

Jean Simmons left England almost immediately afterwards to join not only her husband-to-

IN *So Long at the Fair* (1950) AS THE ENGLISH ARTIST IN PARIS TRYING TO LOCATE A MAN WHO HAS GONE MISSING AT THE GREAT EXHIBITION OF 1899.

because his father was Dutch, Dirk was always to remain a passionate European.

From *So Long at the Fair*, it was back to murder, this time in high society, and Dirk played a music-hall artiste who could well have been the killer of *The Woman in Question*. It now began to look to Dirk as though Rank were deliberately throwing their worst scripts at him and this one could not be saved even by its distinguished director, Anthony Asquith. 'I was terrified of him,' Dirk recalled, 'because he really had an

be, Stewart Granger, but also that band of British actors (James Mason, Deborah Kerr, David Niven and many others) who had now made California a permanent home for these last survivors of the Hollywood Raj. For Dirk, with his Rank contract, there was no chance to join them; nor did he ever really want to do so. Even when he did decide in years to come that he too had to live and work abroad, there was never any thought of America; perhaps

American actor in mind before Rank forced me on him. He was always polite but not wildly enthusiastic and I soon realized that I was not what he wanted ... things improved during the shooting, however, and sometimes he would make me play a scene five or eight different ways, always with that gentle, ironic smile. He told me it amused him to see how rapidly I could "shift gears", as he called it, and give a completely different performance. It was hard to do but stood me in marvellous stead in the time to come. That was the great

adaptation of Anouilh's *Eurydice* in which Dirk played the Orpheus figure, a vagrant musician who meets his fate in Eurydice, played by Mai Zetterling, who also won glowing reviews for a production which broke all records at the Lyric Theatre, Hammersmith.

The role of the bewitched boy overwhelmed by his first love affair, and half in love with death, was peculiarly suited to Dirk's mournfully romantic stage presence and this was precisely the performance that could have launched him on a long West End career as a romantic leading man, had J. Arthur Rank not got first call on his time. Peter Fleming, reviewing for the *Spectator*, noted, 'Orpheus' raptures and regrets present the actor with almost as many difficulties as opportunities but Mr Bogarde never allows this to be seen, and plays a very awkward part with assurance and complete success.' It would be another two years before Dirk returned to the theatre and, although he did not know it then, there were only another three plays left in his future.

J. Arthur Rank, recognizing a potent team when they saw one, lent Zetterling and Bogarde to an independent Pinewood

AS THE PENNILESS STREET MUSICIAN WITH MAI ZETTERLING IN *POINT OF DEPARTURE* (1950), ANOUILH'S UPDATE OF THE ORPHEUS LEGEND SET IN CONTEMPORARY FRANCE.

lesson Asquith taught me: total concentration at all times and an elasticity of ideas. "Always have lots of different hats in the bag," he used to say, "because you can't do much with just one."'

In this incredibly crowded year Dirk still found time to honour the promise he had made Noël Coward that, whatever happened to him in movies, he would not desert the stage altogether. In 1949-50 he appeared in no fewer than four London productions, three of which (*Foxhole in the Parlour*, *Sleep on My Shoulder* and *The Shaughran*) were very short runs in fringe theatres and of no special significance. But the fourth was something else entirely: *Point of Departure* was an English company for *Blackmailed*, in which Dirk lived and died as an army deserter trying to escape. For the *Observer*, C. A. Lejeune reckoned it 'one of the worst British films ever made, trite, slipshod, slow-moving and resolutely mediocre'. At least *The Times* managed to be a bit more forgiving: 'Our sympathy goes out to poor Mr Bogarde who once again finds himself enveloped in a dirty mackintosh, the eternal deserter, eternally on the run.'

Dirk had almost the same role to play in his next picture, *Hunted*, except that it put him in touch for the first, and maybe the last, time in his life with his paternal feelings. It is the story of a young man and a small boy, again on the run, with Dirk as the seaman who is hiding after murdering his wife's lover and Jon Whiteley as the little boy fleeing his hostile foster parents. Nobody knew how to cast the boy until someone remembered hearing a BBC Radio broadcast of a little boy reading a Christmas poem. If he looked anything like his voice, the director Charlie Crichton decided, they'd use him. He turned out to look even better than he sounded: a six- year-old blond angel. He was hired on the spot. Dirk, as he was later to do on *Our Mother's House*, loved working with children and he and little Jon make an affecting pair as they run out of time. As C. A. Lejeune noted in the *Observer*, 'The

discipline involved in playing with and to a child seems to have found new reserves of strength in Dirk Bogarde's acting.'

Dirk was by now living on the Sussex Downs, at Home Farm, which had been Tony Forwood's family home and was now rented by Dirk for a mere £10 a week. He had orchards and three acres of garden and it was here that Dirk rekindled his childhood passion for

WITH THE SIX-YEAR-OLD JON WHITELEY IN *HUNTED* (1952), PLAYING YET ANOTHER TORMENTED KILLER ON THE RUN. JON WAS LATER TO REAPPEAR WITH HIM IN *THE SPANISH GARDENER*.

THE AMERSHAM COUNTRY SQUIRE: A PRESS IMAGE THAT BOTH THE RANK ORGANISATION AND BOGARDE HIMSELF WERE EVER KEEN TO PERPETUATE.

casualty of the war and he had reluctantly agreed to a divorce, which meant that he gave up custody of his son. On his return from the war he had taken Dirk on again as a client and, now alone, he took on more and more of Dirk's personal management. He was already 'tired of finding jobs for lots of dreary actors' and as Dirk's popularity grew, Forwood was more than willing to allow Dirk's affairs to take precedence. Slowly he divested himself of all his other clients.

And, at last, reviewers seemed to wake up to the possibility that Dirk really was here to stay as a leading man. Even so, *The Times* couldn't resist pointing out, 'The British cinema is particularly addicted to the chase motif and Mr Dirk Bogarde is the champion of those who get chased. Indeed, if there was an Olympic cross-town-and-country event for film actors, Mr Bogarde would start as favourite by virtue of the fantastic amount of practice he has had.' The film opened in London in the week of the death of King George VI but even that could not stop it from becoming one of the big money-makers of the year.

Desperate by now to escape from escaping, Dirk embarked on his next film, *Penny Princess* (1952), which was a disastrous attempt to make a film star of

growing things, one that he was later to recall in his book *Great Meadow*. Like *The Go-Between* and *The Shooting Party*, it captured the magic world of childhood as the adults all around him were preparing to go to war.

At this time Tony Forwood was renting a London mews house on his own. His marriage to Glynis Johns had been a

Yolande Donlan, who had triumphed in the West End as the dumb blonde in *Born Yesterday*. She put up her own money for the picture and played the lead as a New York shop-girl inheriting a bankrupt European principality and turning it round by the invention of alcoholic cheese. She might have been better advised to hand this out to the audience rather than showing them the film, in which Bogarde, in a role originally intended for William Holden (presumably until he read the script), was required to be amusing while dressed in striped pyjamas. The *Daily Mail* commented, 'Mr Bogarde, a serious young actor, has a certain amount of trouble trying to be romantically funny in his pyjamas,' and Dirk himself later noted, 'I had just finished *Hunted* and wanted to try my hand at something light. I heard about *Penny Princess* and practically forced the director, Val Guest, to give me a test. The result was terrible.' Much later he was to remark, memorably, '*Penny Princess* was about as funny as a baby's coffin.'

After that little fiasco Dirk was eager to get back to the theatre and the choice was a revival of *The Vortex*, the play in which Noël Coward had scored his original success as author and star in 1924. This was the first major postwar production and Noël himself was happy with it, as he wrote in his diary: 'Extremely good, well directed and played. Dirk Bogarde a little floppy but a fine actor.' Once again Dirk had chosen a dangerous and difficult subject, this time drug addiction and a near-incestuous relationship between a tormented son and

his socialite mother. He was therefore not exactly reassured by Coward's first-night telegram, which read simply: 'Don't worry, dear boy, it all depends on you.' So, if Dirk was making silly or formula films as a contract actor in a not-very-imaginative film company, at least he was stretching his talent when he could, in the theatre, and being appreciated for it by the people who mattered. The problem was that his contract with Rank never really allowed him enough time to develop a meaningful stage career. By the time *The Vortex* moved to the

THE VORTEX, THE PLAY WITH WHICH NOËL COWARD HAD MADE HIS NAME OVERNIGHT IN 1924 AS AUTHOR, DIRECTOR AND STAR, WAS GIVEN A STRONG STAGE REVIVAL IN 1952 WITH ISOBEL JEANS AS THE MOTHER AND DIRK AS THE DRUG-ADDICTED, OBSESSIVE SON.

Criterion Theatre from the Lyric Hammersmith, Dirk had been replaced by Michael Gough and was already back at work in front of the camera.

Nineteen fifty-two ended with *The Gentle Gunman*, yet another 'sensitive criminal' role, though this time the story was of two Irish brothers (the other was played by John Mills) sent to London during the war by the IRA. Dirk was the fanatic and Mills the peace-keeper and reviews were rather better than for Dirk's last few films. But what was really good about *The Gentle Gunman* was that it spared Dirk from one of J. Arthur Rank's regular purges. With the local film industry already severely threatened by Hollywood imports, Rank had decided to make sweeping cut-backs in the number of their contract artists and the only thing that spared Dirk from the fate suffered by countless starlets was that he happened already to have signed for *The Gentle Gunman*. Even after he had made twelve films for them, Rank still had no particular interest in Dirk and virtually no appreciation of his talent at all. All that was to change, however, with his next picture, *Appointment in London*.

For the first time Dirk's reviews were not just lukewarm or uncritical but personally triumphant. The *Daily Telegraph* noted, 'Mr Bogarde, happily escaping at last from the world of spivs and crooks, now steps into the front rank of English screen actors,' and the *Daily Mail* even found a woman in the audience to add, 'That man can act with his skin.' The story of a young airman in Bomber Command who, against orders, joins a major offensive against the Germans was, in the view of the *Sunday Graphic*, 'Mr Bogarde's finest hour. Whether discreetly conveying the inward and spiritual grace of a born leader or the outward and visible signs of a young lover,

PERFECTING HIS TORTURED CRIMINAL IN *THE GENTLE GUNMAN* (1952).

he never once slops over into implausibility.' Fame, or at least respect, at last.

But despite the relative success of *The Gentle Gunman*, Dirk was still not getting any respect from the Rank Organisation because he was not seen as a money-maker for them. He was deeply hurt by their refusal to allow him any role in an important studio project. His films so far had never made real profits and he was not considered 'box-office' enough to be included in the cast for *The Cruel Sea*. As a result, even when he had a hit with *Appointment in London*, none of his masters at Rank had even bothered to watch it. But they did react to the increasingly enthusiastic press attention. Reading the reviews of *Appointment in London*, and the film that followed it, *Desperate Moments* (yet another prisoner on the run), finally persuaded them that with a bit more effort on their part they might have a money-making star in Dirk after all. Things were about to improve.

They started with *They Who Dare*, a war movie about soldiers on a dangerous mission, directed by Lewis Milestone, who had made *All Quiet on the Western Front*. Although the film was eventually dismissed by the press as 'How Dare They?', Milestone was a Hollywood director of real quality and Dirk, on a difficult mountain-climbing location in Cyprus, was

treated to a master class in screenwriting and acting from one of the best in the business. While they were on that location the producer, Betty Box, in the middle of a long journey from Scotland to London, happened to be changing trains at Crewe. On the station platform bookstall, she picked up a comic novel by a young man who was just completing his medical training. It was called *Doctor in the House*.

APPOINTMENT IN LONDON, THE FILM WHICH AFFORDED HIM AT LAST AN ESCAPE FROM GENTLE GUNMEN AND LITTLE BOYS LOOKING FOR GOD. 'BOGARDE IS NOW THE FOREMOST YOUNG ACTOR ON THE BRITISH SCREEN' (PICTUREGOER).

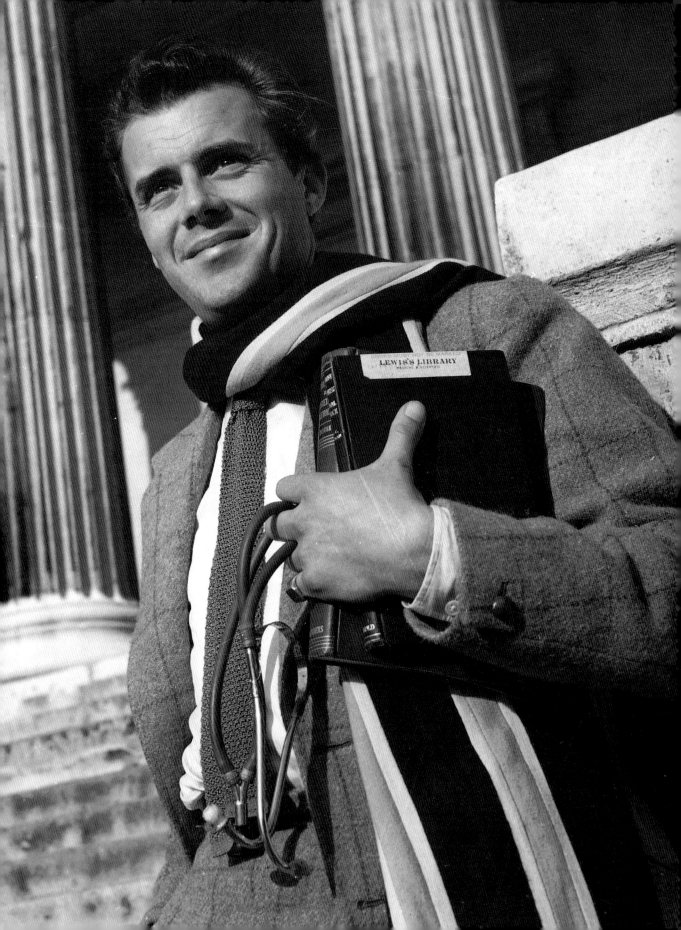

4 DOCTOR IN DEMAND

'It doesn't mean a thing to be known as the "most successful" or "the most highly paid" film star.'

Up to this point, although he had played plenty of the kind of antiseptic love scenes so beloved of fifties filmgoers, Dirk was not considered a conventionally sexy romantic lead. Perhaps because the producer, Betty Box, was a woman she saw Dirk as no one else ever had, as a heartthrob with the kind of offbeat sincerity and sexual allure that in the United States baffled male audiences about Frank Sinatra. Sinatra too was skinny and not, apparently, physically prepossessing. Like Dirk, he had nothing of the Victor Mature, Cornel Wilde beefcake that seemed to be in fashion. Nevertheless, the girls adored him and the same was true of Dirk. But not until *Doctor in the House*.

The rights to the novel had been available cheap for several months but it wasn't until Betty Box took them up that the idea for a film version was mooted. Dirk was cast as a young doctor completing his training at a major London teaching hospital (in reality University College Hospital). Dr Simon Sparrow and his fellow students have many romantic and medical comic adventures on their way to final qualifications, not all of them connected with the frightening senior surgeon, Sir Lancelot Spratt. The film was an unprecedented hit.

Although Dirk had had grave doubts about playing what was effectively the straight man around the wards, he had luckily been persuaded by Tony Forwood that this was the role to get him away from spivs and Service heroes for ever. Both Betty Box and her director, Ralph Thomas, had a tough time convincing the Rank executives that, on the single dismal experience of *Penny Princess*, Dirk could play light comedy and, as he wrote later, 'There is no question in my mind whatsoever that

AUTOGRAPH-HUNTING AT THE 1954 THEATRICAL GARDEN PARTY.

BOGARDE · PAVLOW · MORE · SINDEN

COLOUR BY TECHNICOLOR

DOCTOR in the HOUSE

also starring KAY KENDALL · JAMES ROBERTSON JUSTICE · DONALD HOUSTON

Adapted from his own novel by RICHARD GORDON · Screenplay by NICHOLAS PHIPPS · Directed by RALPH THOMAS · Produced by BETTY E. BOX

THE ORIGINAL TEAM OF YOUNG
DOCTORS IN 1954. THIRTY
YEARS LATER, THE SERIES THEY
HAD STARTED FOR THE WIDE
SCREEN WAS STILL HAPPILY
RUNNING AS A SMALL-SCREEN
TELEVISION WEEKLY SITCOM.

if they had not taken this courageous stand I should never have had a career in the cinema at all. It was the absolute turning point, and by their action they secured me in my profession, a debt it is impossible to repay.'

As usual, the Rank Organisation didn't know what they had got: essentially the start of one of the longest-running film, and then television, series in the history of popular entertainment. With the explosion of hospital dramas in recent years it's hard to credit that the first reason for their nervousness was a widely-held belief that films about doctors were death at the box office. Accordingly, in the publicity stills the team were ordered to wear sports jackets. Rank gave Betty Box a very low shooting budget and told her she was only allowed to use their few remaining contract artists.

Among them she found not only Dirk but also Kenneth More, just coming off the triumph of *Genevieve*, Donald Sinden, who had played the part Dirk so wanted in *The Cruel Sea*, and Donald Houston. Box and Thomas also cast Shirley Eaton as the love interest. Eaton had been, until this, a totally conventional Rank starlet, always the dumb blonde. In *Doctor in the House* she was allowed to discover beneath the blonde mane and the mammary glands a talent for comedy. With the addition of James Robertson Justice as the apoplectic Sir Lancelot Spratt, the mythical St Swithin's Hospital was where every moviegoer wanted to have his or her appendix out.

Donald Sinden recalled the sheer fun of making the movie. 'We were all young and exuberant and Dirk, already sporting his first status symbol, a Rolls-Royce, had discovered that the left side of his face was far more attractive than the right, so he always secured for himself the correct position on the screen ... With no great optimism the Rank Organisation subjected the film to a sneak

'MR BOGARDE, WEARING A
YOUTHFULLY LOST LOOK,
DISPLAYS A GIFT FOR COMEDY
I DON'T RECALL HAVING EVER
SEEN BEFORE IN HIM'
(*THE STAR*).

THE ORIGINAL YOUNG DOCTORS: DONALD HOUSTON, DONALD SINDEN, KENNETH MORE AND A PENSIVE DIRK.

WITH RALPH THOMAS, THE DIRECTOR, ON THE SET OF *DOCTOR IN THE HOUSE* JUST AFTER THE SHOOTING OF THE RAG – HENCE DIRK'S UNUSUALLY DISHEVELLED LOOK.

preview at a suburban cinema. A small group of us sat in the circle and *Doctor in the House* flashed on to the screen. It was soon being greeted with ecstatic laughter. We were a hit.' Indeed, when James Robertson Justice asked Dirk, as they examined a patient, 'What's the bleeding time?' and Dirk replied, 'Half past two, sir,' the laugh was so loud that it drowned the whole of the next scene. The film created a remarkable record by being seen by more people in its first year on release than any other in British cinema history. Seventeen million tickets were sold, one for every two potential filmgoers in the entire nation. Even the Rankery was impressed.

The success of *Doctor in the House* shot

Dirk way up in the box-office charts, where he was to remain for the next decade. But, as Dirk recalled, that didn't leave much time for training in what was still for him a relatively new medium. And he had started more or less at the top. 'I was raw edges for twelve years. I did what I was told,' Dirk said later, but he learned to be a screen actor from his crew when he was already a big star.

DIRK AT LAST LEARNING THE
TECHNIQUES OF LIGHTING AND
FILMING WHICH HE HAD SPENT
HIS FIRST FILM DECADE
BLISSFULLY IGNORING.

His education started quite by accident. One day he was sitting on the set when he noticed Bob Thompson, his camera operator, staring at him. When asked what was up Thompson answered, honestly, 'I was wondering how the fuck you've lasted. You don't know a bloody thing.' Bogarde recalls: 'So I asked him, "What don't I know?" and he said, "Nothing. You don't know a bloody thing. You don't know anything about the job, do you?" And I said, "No." He said, "How many frames per second?" "I don't know." "Do you know what an inky dink is?" "No, I don't." "A boom?" "No." "A 75?" "No." "A 4?" "No." "Well, you don't know anything." And on we went, over and over, of course behind the director's back always.'

It was the beginning of a master class in film technique which Dirk was to continue right up to the end of his British film career and which laid the groundwork for his remarkable sequence of European movies twenty years later. He learned which lights did what, how to work with the camera, where to look to produce the best effect, how to act with a white chalk line on the studio floor indicating where the other actors stood when their schedules didn't accord with his, and the millions of other details about film-making that he had somehow never been told before. 'I was taught by my crew, not my directors.'

His voice was another problem. 'I had to do that myself, nobody ever told me. I heard it and was offended. Oh Christ, you can't talk like that! Oh yes you do, that's how you sound, and so it had to be dealt with. I had to bring my voice down because recording was very bad in those days and it was very light. I trained myself (with the help of Bob Thompson and others) to be a screen actor and when the people in the wardrobe department or the hairdressing department say in amazement, "He doesn't *do* anything with his face," well, I *don't* do anything with my face if you are not looking, but I do everything if you are.'

One of the greatest lessons was actually learned in the Rank canteen, where Dirk had already received a note from David Lean asking him not to walk around so arrogantly, but where also, one lunchtime, he found himself sitting next to a group of Alan Ladd's Hollywood technicians over on location. 'We were at Pinewood. I had the star table — well, of course, I would, I was the King of Pinewood in those days — and Alan Ladd was over because things were folding in America, and he was doing a film, I think it was called *The Black Knight*, and they used to sit at the table next to

mine and send him up all the way through lunch, because he always came in a bit late because he always went to see his dailies at a different time to me. He came in, clattered down in his "knight without armour" or chain-mail thing and they'd been saying really bloody things about him behind his back at this table. It was all his friends, I might say, all his mates, his stand-in, his double, his stunt double. One of them said, "Watch this, watch this!" and said, "Hi, Alan, watcha do today then?" and there was a great silence at the table and Alan just stood and looked at them and said, "I did a great look," and I

1955 STUDIO PORTRAITS AS RANK NOW TRIED TO PLACE HIM IN THE GREAT OUTDOORS.

thought, That's it! If you can do one great look, you're halfway in.'

Soon enough Dirk had perfected his own 'great look'. 'It's clear that I did have a form of sex appeal, certainly for what we called the teenagers before the Beatles came in and before there were pop stars. I was always in the first ten at the box office. Always first or second, always, for a number of years. I think it was the kind of films I did. You know, little boy looking for God, staunch upper lip, brave captains. I took care to look pretty. Now the fact that I was as scrawny as a plucked hen, and a skinny hen at that, didn't seem to matter. The Rank Organisation did supply me with dumb-bells and great sets of wheels I was supposed to do that with, and all I did was put on two sweaters, and then put on my shirt, and then put on my jacket, so everything was attained in that way. But it didn't matter. People didn't mind me being scrawny. And I'm not an idiot. I was totally aware that the English hero in movies was usually dressed in tweeds and a Pringle V-neck sweater and always baggy trousers. Now that wasn't my scene and it wasn't for my audience and I switched that around. I leaped into black leather. In an instant we sold 10,000 pairs of trousers in the King's Road. Well, I learned from that, and particularly women in audiences don't quite know what nerve has been hit, they know that they find you attractive but they don't quite know why. The cinema is a sexual thing. You go to the movies for sex. You may not go there to watch a porno movie, I don't mean that kind of thing, but it is a sexual excitement. I knew the reaction I was getting to my work and to being who I was, that people were turned on by me. When I was young, I'm talking about, not now, and there was an alchemy at work and so I used it. The whole thing is fake, but then that's what sex is, it's an illusion. That's what the cinema is, it's an illusion. But I was jolly sure that I was going to make every wing commander I played as mischievous, as flirty, as physically attractive as I could. I was totally aware of it and when I realized that I was "working" on screen, which I only did about three years afterwards, I wasn't a very good actor but something was happening and then I nursed it. I had a special little light for my eyes, it was called a "bar". Dirk's bar or Bogarde's bar — nobody else had it. I had it, because the only thing I had that was a good feature was my eyes.

'You've got to work at your charm, you've got to work at your sex appeal. But there has to come a time when all of that has to stop. You put on your Barratt's shoes and Barratt's hat and creep around the house as *The Servant*. But I had all that, I had it. I'm very glad. Nice while it lasted.'

At the height of his popularity it was suggested to Dirk that there was an American director in retreat from the communist-baiting House UnAmerican Activities Committee in the United States Congress who was no longer able to work in Hollywood because of his left-wing political views and who might be able to get backing for his next film if only he had a major British star. Bogarde grudgingly agreed to look at one of his films, which he did one snowy afternoon in his private screening room at Pinewood. In true movie-star fashion, he arrived several hours late. A tall figure in a shabby raincoat asked Dirk if he could accompany him to the screening and Dirk refused, leaving the American standing in the snow.

The film he saw was *The Prowler*, with Van Heflin and Evelyn Keyes. 'I had never seen that kind of a film before. I mean, except for French films or German films, and I suddenly thought: My God, I can be in this. This is what this man does. I didn't care whether it was a good, bad or indifferent film. It was a wonderfully composed, wonderfully shot, excitingly photographed piece of work and people looked real and things looked real and that was what I was never able to do in my movies. I never looked real in anything. And this guy was standing out in the snow and after the first reel was over, twenty minutes, I knew that was my destiny. So I went out, brought him in. We sat down together and I said, "I'm going to do your script whatever," and we got terribly pissed at the bar because [my agreeing to do his movie meant] he got his money.'

Dirk invited him inside and there began a friendship and partnership that was to last for the rest of their lives. The director's name was Joseph Losey. It wasn't an easy friendship, for the two men were out of sympathy with each other's politics. 'Dirk, in so far as he understood any of my political opinions, certainly didn't agree with them, so it took much courage and much acceptance to perform the unselfish act of faith which he did,' said Losey. Bruised and battered by his rejection by the Hollywood establishment of which he had

been a part, he was a wounded man and he found the eccentricities of the English maddening even when Dirk had provided the wherewithal, by his enthusiastic acceptance of the leading role, for him to work in England. Their first film together was difficult for them both. 'On *The Sleeping Tiger*,' Losey wrote of his start in British cinema, 'I worked anonymously and without knowledge of British idiosyncrasies and with little confidence except what Dirk gave me.' He was still haunted by his Hollywood past. Dirk was understanding and not a little excited by the cloak-and-dagger elements. 'And then the problems started because he told me what McCarthyism meant — that he was on the black list and that he was known as Victor

IN *THE SLEEPING TIGER*, THE 1954 FILM THAT FIRST BROUGHT DIRK TOGETHER WITH JOE LOSEY, WHO WAS THEN HAVING TO WORK UNDER THE PSEUDONYM VICTOR HANBURY.

Hanbury, and I said, "I know Victor Hanbury and you don't look anything like him," so he said, "I don't have to look — but Victor Hanbury will be sitting in a chair with 'Director' marked on the back of it and he will be the director on the credits and on everything and I do not exist, so will you please remember that?" So that was fine. I could play that game too, I'd been in Intelligence all through the war. We were spotted once by Ginger Rogers' mother. Ginger was over here too, doing a movie with Stanley Baker, in the same studio and Ginger Rogers' mother was a very tough cookie — and she saw Joe and me together and said, "That's Joe Losey!" and she was adamant. We had to move him. I had to hide him in the back of my car, under two travelling rugs, with all his luggage and take him to a hotel at Windsor and we had to go through traffic and down side-streets and alleys and through lanes. You can't imagine the persecution that was on.'

It was a good thing she didn't hang around long enough to recognize another McCarthy refugee, Carl Foreman, who was also working on the film. The script is credited to one Derek Frye but was, in fact, written by Foreman and Harold Buchman. It wasn't Foreman's greatest hour, given the subsequent comments on the script from both the critics and those involved in the movie, but he later became one of America's leading writer-producer-directors.

In *The Sleeping Tiger* Dirk reverted to his usual role of neurotic criminal, this time the guinea pig of a criminologist-doctor who kidnaps him in order to use him in his experiments. Dirk has a steamy affair with the doctor's wife, the delectable Alexis Smith, and then abandons her to cooperate with the doctor. What was different this time was Losey's taut, dark shooting, his flawless composition and his unerring instinct for the right angle. 'With this film, in fact,' Robert Ottaway wrote for the *Sunday Graphic*, 'Bogarde graduates from the class of feather-weight heroes.' Dirk himself, however, was less impressed. 'We thought the script itself was frightful and it embarrassed us terribly to have to do it,'

and the *News Chronicle* agreed: 'With a better script it might have been an exciting and unusual film.'

Losey thought it had 'no real promise and didn't hang together' but his gloom may be attributed to his circumstances. 'I was working on a closed set, where I was not supposed to be directing the picture I was directing and everybody knew I was and was being paid peanuts for — and was glad to do it, too.' Nevertheless, Bogarde had by now found the director with whom in the future much of his best work would be done. But it was to be nearly ten years before they worked together again.

For his next film Bogarde went back to a script he had first played in the live theatre in 1948, the domestic comedy *For Better for Worse*. His co-stars included Susan Stephen as his young wife and the redoubtable Athene Seyler. Dennis Price had a small role, as did Thora Hird. Sidney James, later to be much more famous as Sid James, had such a small role that his character didn't even have a name. He is described as simply 'The Foreman'. But Dirk was, of course, the leading man and his previous knowledge of the role gave him a depth that this frothy piece didn't really merit. His reward here was a review in the *Evening Standard* announcing that 'Bogarde strikes me as one of the three best young actors in British films,' but infuriatingly, the critic neglected to share with his readers the identity of the other two. In any case, the *Doctor* pictures notwithstanding, comedy was never Dirk's forte.

From now on Dirk's personal reviews would usually be better than those for the film in which he was currently appearing. As these were still J. Arthur Rank contract jobs, he had no freedom to stay with a maverick director like Losey and essentially very little freedom in the choice of roles he played. But at least he was now never at a loss for work and the general critical amazement that he could play comedy for the *Doctor* series and hunted criminals everywhere else did him

WITH CECIL PARKER, EILEEN HERLIE AND SUSAN STEPHEN IN *FOR BETTER FOR WORSE* (1954).

nothing but good. Through the middle 1950s he remained regularly high on all box-office charts almost regardless of the film he had just made.

For Better for Worse was followed immediately by *The Sea Shall Not Have Them*, in which Dirk played a flight sergeant trapped in a dinghy with Michael Redgrave after bailing out over the Channel. The film is best remembered now for an early feminist protest by the actresses in the Rank stable, all of whom signed an open letter to their bosses complaining bitterly that the studio was still making far too many war films with no roles for them. When the film reached the Odeon, Leicester Square, the neon sign read: 'MICHAEL REDGRAVE DIRK BOGARDE in THE SEA SHALL NOT HAVE THEM.' Noël Coward, glancing up as he crossed the square, was heard to murmur, 'I don't see why not — everybody else has.' When Dirk got to hear of this funny but barbed comment, relations between

WITH MICHAEL REDGRAVE IN *THE SEA SHALL NOT HAVE THEM* (1954). 'MY MAIN QUARREL HERE IS THE MISUSE OR NON-USE OF STAR TALENT. REDGRAVE MAY BE A VIP IN THE SCRIPT BUT HE IS A NONENTITY IN THE DINGHY WHILE BOGARDE, WHO CAN THRILL OR AMUSE US AT WILL, SPENDS MOST OF HIS TIME JUST GRIZZLING' (*DAILY SKETCH*).

the two old friends were a bit strained.

By now at the top of Rank's salary scale, Dirk had been able to buy a mansion in Buckinghamshire that was much used by his publicists to picture him as a landed gentleman seen variously in jodhpurs, playing with his dogs, in the saddle or propping up his Bentley. Fan magazines of the time emphasized the gentle bachelorhood of it all. This was not, of course, the whole truth; Forwood was never mentioned, even though they were now sharing their living quarters, but Dirk found this country image useful to offset any other questions about his private life. He dated a number of actresses, none of them for long enough to cause him or them any disquiet and most of them hand-picked by the studio in a copycat version of what the Hollywood moguls had offered him at the start of his career. What had then seemed so onerous was now a convenient way to adjust his public and private life.

But Hollywood was now showing for the first time real interest in Dirk. Indeed every time he turned down *The Egyptian* (a biblical spectacular in which the role finally went to Edmund Purdom) Dirk noted with pride that the money was doubled. They thought him hard to get. The reality was that he was stuck with his seven-year commitment to Rank, who, on the rare occasions when he went back to the theatre, would simply add the time lost on to the end of his contract. Tony Forwood had driven a hard bargain on the latest contract, winning for Dirk the rare honour of script approval, although it was not of much use

as there were precious few scripts around to approve.

The next Rank contract job was *Simba*, a drama of Mau Mau terrorists in Kenya. This got off to a very uneasy start when the director, Brian Desmond Hurst, and his crew unaccountably set off to film all the African locations without any of the cast. They simply took extras in the vague hope that these could be matched up with the stars back at Pinewood. The only problem with this scheme was that they were hoping to get Jack Hawkins for the leading role. When he subsequently proved unavailable, they turned to Dirk, only to find that the

WITH VIRGINIA MCKENNA IN *SIMBA* (1955), THE STORY OF SETTLERS IN KENYA AT THE TIME OF THE MAU MAU TERROR. 'BOGARDE HAS ONE OF THOSE TAUT, TRUCULENT, ANTI-PATHETIC PARTS WHICH HE PLAYS WITH BEAUTIFUL PRECISION AND GOES ON PLAYING TIME AFTER TIME' (*SUNDAY EXPRESS*).

double they had used in Africa was the perfect height for Hawkins but several inches too tall for Dirk. They then went on a frantic search for another actor to play the police inspector. Again, they had used a blond double in Africa, only to find when they returned a total absence of young blond leading men on the studio roster or indeed anywhere else. This problem was eventually solved by telling Donald Sinden to go and get his hair dyed blond by lunchtime.

Reviews were largely negative and it was Derek Monsey for the *Sunday Express* who was the first to pinpoint Bogarde's real problem at this time: 'Bogarde has one of those taut, truculent, antipathetic parts which he plays with beautiful precision. And goes on playing time after time. Yet, given the opportunity, he can play comedy, he can play the lover, and he can play intelligent, sensitive parts. Among the young British stars he is that rare animal, a very fine actor. But you can kill the best actor or the topmost star with too many stereotyped and unsympathetic parts. The problem is — can Bogarde survive?'

For the time being, the answer was yes. At the end of 1954 Dirk made the second of his four Simon Sparrow films, *Doctor at Sea*, this one mainly interesting for marking Brigitte

Bardot's debut in the British cinema. Bogarde was now getting around £10,000 per picture. Bardot got £750 for a role already rejected by Kay Kendall and although she sulked over the formula script, Dirk grew very fond of her and during the shooting wrote in *Picturegoer*, 'Bardot was like a breath of Oklahoma on the set every day. The kind of sex she suggests is

warm, uninhibited, completely natural. With her superb figure, long legs and flowing hair, she has a gazelle-like grace. The effect? Pure enchantment.'

But he went on to write accurately enough about her future career: 'Even without her French accent, Brigitte would be too much for British studios to handle. You see, Brigitte takes the trouble to put across sex as an art. For most of our girls it's a farce.'

The formula for *Doctor at Sea* was pretty much as before: James Robertson

WITH BARDOT AND DIRECTOR RALPH THOMAS ON THE SET OF *DOCTOR AT SEA*. 'DIRK BOGARDE TAKES TO THE ROLE OF THE DOCTOR AS IF HE HAD BEEN BORN WITH A STETHOSCOPE IN HIS MOUTH' (*SUNDAY TIMES*).

Justice, the prickly surgeon in *Doctor in the House*, was now a prickly captain of a cargo steamer on which Dr Sparrow was the ship's doctor, with Bardot as their most glamorous passenger. The *Sunday Express* believed that Dirk had now taken to the role of the doctor 'as if he had been born with a stethoscope in his mouth'. But when the film was released Bogarde received more than 500 letters accusing him of 'going off with that French hussy', so for the next film in the series it was hastily arranged that Dr Simon Sparrow would go off with a nice English girl. For the second year running, Dirk was voted the most popular actor on the British screen.

His next picture, *Cast a Dark Shadow* (originally titled *Naked Is the Flame)*, was a routine murder melodrama with Bogarde cast as a pathological charmer who marries a wealthy elderly woman, murders her when he mistakenly believes she is about to alter her will and then makes her death look like an accident. Margaret Lockwood was cast as the blowsy second wife, also a murder prospect, and it was she who took most of the reviews, none of which seemed to have noticed an uneasy resemblance between this script and Emlyn Williams's classic *Night Must Fall*. In any case, the film did little at the box office and even less to arrest contemporary audiences in their headlong flight to the new miracle of television.

As there were no new scripts around of much interest to him, and as he was getting more than slightly bored with the Rank theory that he could either be a comic lover in doctor's disguise or a pathological killer in a raincoat, but virtually nothing in between, Dirk decided, like his audiences in this year of 1955, to move away for a while.

Three years had elapsed since he had last appeared on the stage and the offer this time was more than usually attractive. A young Peter Hall had come to him with *Summertime*, a light romance by the Italian

CAST A DARK SHADOW (1955). 'A BRILLIANTLY DISGUSTING PERFORMANCE FROM DIRK BOGARDE, ALLOWED NOT ONLY TO PLAY A MURDERER FOR ONCE WITHOUT HIS RAINCOAT BUT ALSO TO ACT AS WELL' (*SUNDAY EXPRESS*).

ON LOCATION FOR
THE SPANISH GARDENER
(1956), 'A SLOW, STRANGE FILM
IN WHICH BOGARDE'S BASIC
COMPLEXITY FAILS TO GEL
WITH THE CHARACTER OF A
PEACEFUL EARTHY PEASANT'
(*PICTUREGOER*).

playwright Ugo Betti. The deal was for a long regional tour, on which he was to star opposite Geraldine McEwan and Gwen Ffrangçon Davies, to be followed by a season at the Apollo on Shaftesbury Avenue. The tour was traumatic for Dirk. Every stage door of every town they played was packed with young female fans and when they also started to invade the stalls, calling out, 'We love you, Dirk,' at crucial moments of the plot, Dirk decided reluctantly that the theatre was no longer a safe home, especially since stage fright, always a problem, became almost unbearable because now he was a big star and therefore much more exposed on stage than he had ever been before. 'On the first night, particularly the last play I did in London at the Apollo, I remember saying, "You can't be as frightened as I am now and still be alive.

No way can you be. This is as near death, execution and everything else that I've ever come across." It was much, much more perilous than anything I went through in the war and I went through six years of it. It is terrifying and it never gets better. The only way I can describe it is, without it you can't act and I don't like "acting" as a term, but you can't, shall I say, "perform" without that fear, you do not expose your soul, at the risk of being pretentious, and you do not expose a gut that you have, that you don't even know you have, that you are carrying about as a person. That terror releases a million things in your brain, titchy things in the soul, which come flooding in as a kind of antidote to the poison of terror.'

But he didn't have to shake for too long. Despite its money-making tour, the run at the Apollo proved to be more of a stumble and *Summertime* was over in a few weeks. Dirk was only ever to make one more stage appearance, which would not be for another three years, and even then only in Oxford. He went back, gratefully for once, inside his gilded cage as King of Pinewood and indentured Rank retainer, to a new film script and a remarkable reunion with Jon Whiteley, the little boy whom he had so loved after they starred together in *Hunted*. This time the film was *The Spanish Gardener*, about an embittered British diplomat (Michael Hordern) who becomes so jealous of his son's devotion to the gardener that he has him wrongfully prosecuted for theft. In the original

ON THE COSTA BRAVA AT THE TIME OF *THE SPANISH GARDENER*.

A. J. Cronin story it is quite clear that not only the son but also the father is deeply in love with the gardener (Dirk, in a curious refusal to attempt even a faint Spanish accent) but all that closeted homosexuality was too much for Rank, who stripped the story down and destroyed its subtext, leaving Dirk trying to hint at it through the gaps in his lines.

Some time later that year, a new chief executive at Rank, John Davis, who would soon be the most powerful man in British cinema, took Dirk out to lunch and reassured him that, despite appearances to the contrary, manifested in the stream of terrible scripts and directors he had been offered recently, the studio was right behind him and would even allow him to work in Hollywood if the right film came along. Until it did, however, Dirk was more than a little alarmed to read a column by Milton Shulman about the 4,000 film distributors who had taken part in an annual popularity poll. Shulman didn't think much of them or, apparently, of Bogarde: 'These experts have seriously voted Dirk Bogarde as the man who brings more money into British box offices than any other star in the world ... if this poll really reflects the thinking of either the Cinema Managers or the British Public

ON AND OFF THE SET WITH JON WHITELEY, WITH WHOM HE HAD FIRST WORKED IN *HUNTED*. 'THE PARTNERSHIP IS JUST AS EFFECTIVE AS IT WAS THEN, BUT WATCH BOGARDE'S WORK, HIS GENTLE SMILE AND NATURAL DIGNITY AND YOU'LL KNOW WHY HE NOW RATES SO HIGH IN THE STAR ROSTER' (*NEWS OF THE WORLD*).

then few will mourn that cinemas have been closing at the rate of some two hundred a year.'

Nineteen fifty-six ended with yet another war picture, Powell and Pressburger's *Ill Met by Moonlight*. It was based on Major Patrick Leigh Fermor's memoirs of a group of irregular secret agents smuggling a German general from Crete to Egypt. As the major, Dirk did his usual workmanlike job, toiling hard at what was for the most part a formula movie. As often happened, the critics noticed. 'In spite of a ghastly moustache,' thought the *Daily Mail*, 'Bogarde never beats his chest nor brags of his

ILL MET BY MOONLIGHT (1957). 'IN SPITE OF THAT AWFUL MOUSTACHE, BOGARDE DOES WELL AS THE DASHING KIDNAPPER' (*DAILY MAIL*).

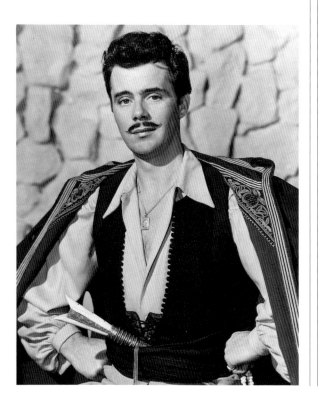

bravery. Indeed, he has the courage to show himself worried, weary and frightened.'

These personal reviews for yet another ho-hum movie stirred up Dirk's frustration. He started again to petition Rank, in person and through Tony Forwood, for better vehicles, for films which would be worthy of the actor he had by now publicly shown himself to be. His restraint was formidable, however, as he continued to make films for Rank that he knew were unworthy of him.

He was always polite on the set, respectful of the technicians who were his teachers, distant but correct with his fellow actors. He never left the set during a day's filming and always remembered to thank those he had worked with at the end of the day. He belonged to a generation where stars knew how to behave and if he was never really close to his colleagues, neither was he ever the object of fear or contempt. Today's megastars, who are isolated in their specially decorated house trailers, surrounded and protected by squads of agents, personal hairdressers, assistants, publicists and the like, who never set foot on the set except for their own scenes and then only at the last minute when the set-up is completed, would not recognize Dirk's kind of stardom. And yet it is certain that he has lasted longer than they will because he took the trouble to know and understand that the medium in which he worked was one of precision teamwork.

For want of anything more exciting, Dirk climbed back into his white coat for his third Dr Simon Sparrow outing, *Doctor at Large*, which seemed to be made up of

random episodes of medical life rather than having the benefit of a single coherent plot. Donald Sinden rejoined the team with the indispensable James Robertson Justice back as Sir Lancelot Spratt from the first movie, his sojourn as a ship's captain now forgotten. They had a starry supporting cast to draw attention away from the gaps in the plot. Dirk now felt the need to defend the series from its more highbrow and irritable critics. 'I know they are not great works of art, but they are enormous fun to make and have a vast family audience appeal. They are entertaining, which after all, is the essence of my job. They have taught me the main essentials about comedy and playing and timing for a cinema audience. If it were not for Dr Sparrow, I probably would not be where I am today. For that, and the foresight of producer Betty Box, who practically forced me to play in the first of the series, I shall be forever grateful.'

Less grateful was the critic Milton Shulman, then of the *Sunday Express*: 'A series which began as a healthy romp about medical students is now scraping the floor of the operating theatre for its comic material.'

It was another six years before Dr Sparrow was sent for again.

BACK TO ST SWITHIN'S FOR THE THIRD TIME, IN *DOCTOR AT LARGE*: SHIRLEY EATON AND SOME REAL-LIFE NURSES ON LOCATION AT UNIVERSITY COLLEGE HOSPITAL IN 1956.

5 REGRETS

'Losing the chance to play T. E. Lawrence was undoubtedly the worst disappointment of my entire career.'

The producer-director team of Betty Box and Ralph Thomas, who had always taken an almost parental interest in Dirk's professional fortunes, now respected a promise they had long made not to leave him in hospital for the rest of his life. Instead, the makers of the *Doctor* series now turned to the great outdoors for *Campbell's Kingdom*, an adventure epic of fire, oil, dynamite and flood. Dirk played a dying visitor come to Canada to take over his grandfather's inheritance in the Rocky Mountains. Filmed on location, with Italy standing in for Canada and the Dolomites as a substitute for the mighty Rockies, the picture also starred Stanley Baker and Michael Craig standing in for themselves. It was one of the first films made on a British budget to challenge Hollywood on its own rough-and-tumble terms. Dams burst, corruption rears its ugly head in the town and in a last-scene miracle Dirk even discovers that all his outdoor heroics have mysteriously cured his illness.

The most intriguing review came from the playwright John Osborne, guest-reviewing in the *Evening Standard*: 'Mr Bogarde is a very good actor with immense personal charm. For years he has been Britain's most popular screen actor during which time he has never appeared in a good film. This is an interesting phenomenon and it could be deduced that his enormous public actually prefer to see him in mediocre films. However, as they have never been given the opportunity to see him in anything else it is impossible to prove this.'

Ironically, Bogarde was unable to accept the proffered role of Jimmy Porter in the film adaptation of Osborne's seminal Royal Court sensation, *Look Back*

OPPOSITE: 'DIRK'S BAR', THE SPECIAL LIGHT FOR HIS EYES, IS MUCH IN EVIDENCE IN THIS 1955 STUDIO PORTRAIT. BELOW: ON THE SET OF *CAMPBELL'S KINGDOM* WITH STANLEY BAKER.

CAMPBELL'S KINGDOM. 'MR BOGARDE IS A VERY GOOD ACTOR WITH IMMENSE PERSONAL CHARM. FOR YEARS HE HAD BEEN BRITAIN'S MOST POPULAR SCREEN ACTOR WITHOUT EVER APPEARING IN A GOOD FILM; THIS IS AN INTERESTING PHENOMENON, AND IT COULD WELL BE THAT HIS ENORMOUS PUBLIC PREFERS TO SEE HIM IN MEDIOCRE FILMS' (*EVENING STANDARD*).

in Anger. He was keen to do it but John Davis and his gang at Rank returned the script to Dirk with a sharp note to the effect that there was altogether too much dialogue. Richard Burton got the role instead. When, a few weeks later, Dirk came upon the Alan Sillitoe novel *Saturday Night and Sunday Morning* and again begged the studio to make it with him, Rank's executives asked how anybody could even consider making a film which began with a forty-year-old woman inducing an abortion in a hot bath. That film would also be made independently a couple of years later and Albert Finney would this time get the role Bogarde had so wanted. If either of these parts had come his way it is possible that Dirk would not have eventually felt he had to move to the European cinema in search of rewarding roles.

But in the meantime a project had come up which was to give Dirk the first of all his greatest hopes to date for his career and then his greatest disappointment. Anthony Asquith, one of the best of Britain's postwar directors, had persuaded his friend, the playwright Terence Rattigan, to write the screenplay of a film about Lawrence of Arabia. They scouted locations, set up a budget with the Rank Organisation and had several exploratory meetings with Dirk, who was to play the mystic soldier and traveller. At one of these Bogarde plucked

up his courage to ask Asquith a very personal question about Lawrence. 'Tell me, really and truly, now we have it all before us, was Lawrence homosexual?' Asquith's face was a study in horror. After a moment he simply replied, 'Not practising.'

A budget of just over £1 million was agreed, other roles were cast and then, less than a month before principal shooting was to start in Arabia, Rank sent for Asquith and Bogarde to tell them that they were pulling the plug on the entire project. No explanation was given and this refusal to explain gave rise to a number of theories. One was that the budget had simply terrified them; another was that the King of Iraq, where they were planning to shoot, had just himself been shot, and the final one was that American co-funders would not proceed with Bogarde in the lead on the principle that he would not be able to carry so ambitious a project into American box offices when he was not even a transatlantic Brit. Another, still more sinister, theory was that the Rank Organisation, having profited considerably in recent months as distributors of *The Bridge on the River Kwai*, now had no wish

THE COUNTRY SQUIRE IN FAINT NEED OF A HAIRCUT, AMERSHAM, 1957.

to annoy the director David Lean or the producer Sam Spiegel, who were apparently already involved in a rival Lawrence project.

Whatever the real cause, Dirk was out of the picture. Rattigan withdrew his script and converted it into a stage play for Alec Guinness called *Ross*. Spiegel and Lean persevered with their *Lawrence* and it finally reached the cinema with Peter O'Toole in 1962. Bogarde still regards this

as his greatest screen disappointment and once again, had it happened, it would surely have been the door to world audiences which he was still fervently seeking.

But for the moment he dutifully exchanged his tight military jodhpurs for even tighter breeches in the Ralph Thomas remake of *A Tale of Two Cities*. His Sidney Carton was subtle, subdued and elegant and his final heroic death on the guillotine was described by the *News Chronicle* as 'a far, far better thing than he has ever done before'. Rank, finally convinced of the restlessness of one of their few remaining contract artists and the one who was still making them the most money, had promised Dirk that he would have to play no more criminals on the run or Little England pictures which had no real chance in the world market. Starting with this *Tale of Two Cities*, Dirk's pictures would henceforth be wide-screen, big-budget spectaculars, which would at least have a fighting chance at the American box office. But his reviews for Sidney Carton were by no means unanimous: Milton Shulman, for the *Sunday*

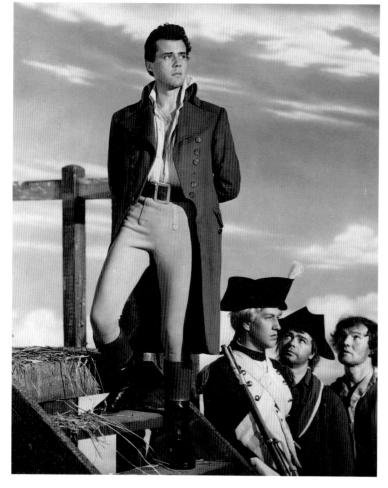

'IT IS A FAR, FAR BETTER THING
I DO NOW THAN I HAVE EVER
DONE BEFORE' . . . DIRK GOING
TO THE SCAFFOLD IN
REMARKABLY TIGHT BREECHES
FOR THE 1958 *A TALE OF
TWO CITIES*.

THE WIND CANNOT READ (1958): 'ONE OF THE FIRST FILMS SINCE BOGARDE WAS GIVEN THE RIGHT, AFTER YEARS OF SPECIALIZING IN MEDIOCRITY, TO DEMAND GOOD PARTS IN FILMS WORTH MAKING...BUT HE HAS STILL GOT HIS HOOKS INTO THE PETER PAN RACKET" (SUNDAY EXPRESS).

Express, thought that 'Bogarde misses much of the suave cynicism of Sidney Carton' and Alexander Walker wrote, 'You couldn't really believe his Sidney Carton had ever been a wastrel, for he was such a nicely-spoken young man.'

From the guillotine Dirk went straight into another Box-Thomas production, *The Wind Cannot Read*, a sentimental story of a doomed love affair between a British officer and a young Japanese girl (Yoko Tani), whom he meets at a language school in New Delhi, before going off to fight in Burma, where he is captured and tortured. On his return to India he finds his girl dying of an incurable brain disease, thereby neatly getting the film off the miscegenation hook. At that time it was unthinkable for a white good guy to marry or even be happy with a black or Asian woman, so one of them had to die (as Lieutenant Cable

THE PRODUCER-DIRECTOR TEAM WHO WERE TO REMAIN, ACROSS THE YEARS, LOYAL ALWAYS TO DIRK AND IMMENSELY INFLUENTIAL IN HIS CAREER: BETTY BOX AND RALPH THOMAS.

does in *South Pacific*). Again the reviews were very mixed. One critic noted that 'if the wind could not read, it certainly couldn't write either', while Derek Monsey for the *Sunday Express* felt that 'in this film, where fire, virility, and a positive attack on the officer type are all demanded, he still offers rather too much of the wry smile, the imperceptibly quivering stiff upper lip, the spaniel pathos in the eyes. He is still prowling the screen, demanding mother love from his millions of female fans. Bogarde is honest, sincere, intelligent. But in a film of tragic passion and contemporary significance that is not nearly enough.'

Towards the end of 1958 Dirk made his final appearance as a stage actor. Once again he chose a difficult and demanding play, Jean Anouilh's *Jezebel*, and once again the screaming fans were at the stage door to make his still-reclusive life impossible. The play, which was having its British première at the Oxford Playhouse some twenty-five years after it had been written, was a highly charged drama about an unhappy son in love with an heiress but so humiliated by his parents' poverty that he pretends to be an orphan.

The reviews were not good. *The Times* thought Dirk had 'a fine, nervous fire', but Basil Boothroyd in *Punch* noted, 'As the son, Dirk Bogarde gives a competent acting performance with conscious grace and good looks, where hell and torment are needed.' As usual, the most thoughtful review came from Kenneth Tynan: 'Dirk Bogarde has one expression that is grave and weak, another that is grave and wry, and a capacity for sudden shouting that serves to break the monotony; he rings what changes he can on limited acting resources.'

There were no longer any plans to move *Jezebel* to the West End and it was

DIRK'S LAST APPEARANCE IN A PLAY. ANOUILH'S BOLD *JEZEBEL*, WITH HERMIONE BADDELEY, AT THE OXFORD PLAYHOUSE IN 1958.

with a mixture of relief and regret that Dirk gave up the stage. When, five years later, Laurence Olivier suggested that he might like to open the Chichester Festival Theatre as *Hamlet*, Dirk, perhaps remembering his worsening problem with stage fright, couldn't face it. He 'funked the honour and probably the greatest chance I have ever been offered really to learn my craft'. As with *Lawrence*, the role went to Peter O'Toole.

Dirk was a huge film star and, as usual, equivocal about the meaning of that

apparently innocuous term. 'I didn't like the stardom, I never have, if that's what it was called. I hated it. It stopped me doing the theatre. I lost my nerve in the theatre because of the perfectly sweet fans who used to come screaming to the theatre to see me in a play and they didn't know what the hell they were looking at and they broke up the place and threw meat pies at us and that kind of thing. "We love you, Dirk!" and all that, great, but it ruined the plays, it ruined the company and it ruined what I was trying to do anyway, so I thought: Pack it up.' Once and for all, Dirk was now committed to a film career.

THE STUDIO PORTRAIT WITH WHICH DIRK CLOSED THE 1950S AT RANK.

As a kind of consolation prize for losing *Lawrence*, Anthony Asquith suggested they should film George Bernard Shaw's *The Doctor's Dilemma*. A strong supporting cast included Leslie Caron, Alistair Sim and

Robert Morley in this tale of a Harley Street doctor who, finding a cure for tuberculosis, has to decide whether to use it on a young artist who, though a scoundrel, is also a genius with a fetching wife, or on a nice but otherwise undistinguished colleague. This time the reviews were ecstatic, most importantly in America, where audiences were at last getting to know Dirk. *Time*, writing of *The Doctor's Dilemma*, noted, 'Dirk Bogarde ... best known in the United States as a sort of British Robert Wagner, turns in a remarkably subtle and mature performance as the heroic villain.' All the others were equally favourable, and if Dirk had to keep turning down Hollywood films such as *The Egyptian*, at least they were now being offered by a

WITH PRODUCER ANATOLE DE GRUNWALD AND DIRECTOR ANTHONY ASQUITH ON THE SET OF BERNARD SHAW'S *THE DOCTOR'S DILEMMA* (1959).

Darryl F. Zanuck desperate to replace an ailing Marlon Brando.

Dirk was turning down other projects too. He could have played the role that made an international star of Frenchman Louis Jourdan in *Gigi* if his contract with Rank had not kept him working on their films throughout the shooting period. When he did finally get to America that year it was not to work but to see friends on a brief holiday. He was amused but not thrilled to find his *Tale of Two Cities* being widely advertised as 'Two Men and a Girl in Turbulent Paris'.

Back home again, he was to discover an even greater problem than American hype for British classics in the release of *The Doctor's Dilemma*. Bewildered cinema managers were reporting to Rank a distinctly curious new phenomenon: audiences would arrive at the cinema in large numbers, stand around the foyer and then go home again without ever purchasing a ticket. It didn't take long for someone to work out what was happening. The crowds were turning up to see what they were convinced was the fourth in their beloved *Doctor* series. One look at the stills in the foyer brought home to them the terrible realization that this Shavian period classic did not have Dr Simon Sparrow in its list of characters. Audiences felt mysteriously betrayed and there were some

who never forgave Bogarde for what they regarded as some obscure trick being played on them by a wily film star they thought of as a member of their family.

For his next film Dirk went back to Anthony Asquith, having by now quite recovered from the terror the director had inspired in him during their first film together. Dirk was still expected to display the versatility Asquith had demanded at the beginning but by now he was more than confident that he could deliver it. *Libel* was the culmination of that ability to change character with ease, for it gave Dirk the opportunity to play three separate roles in an otherwise unremarkable courtroom thriller. The film's attraction was the chance not only to work with Asquith again and to display this facility for technical acting but to pull off a showy trick that the newspapers could not fail to notice. 'This is a real actor's performance and a very good one too,' glowed the *Sunday Express*, while the *News Chronicle* said, 'Mr Bogarde's own performance is in the Guinness class.' Praise indeed, as Alec Guinness was already a buzzword for chameleon-like versatility.

THE THREE FACES OF DIRK WITH OLIVIA DE HAVILLAND IN THE 1959 COURTROOM THRILLER *LIBEL*. 'MR BOGARDE'S TRIPLE PERFORMANCE IS IN THE ALEC GUINNESS CLASS' (*NEWS CHRONICLE*).

6 SURVIVING HOLLYWOOD

'A fiasco. I had to beg

my agent to get me

the role of the villain

in HMS Defiant

after Song without

End *was shown.'*

It was dawning on Dirk, at the beginning of 1960, that if he wanted to be an international film star rather than the local boy made good at Rank, sooner or later he would have to go to the centre of moviemaking.

With nothing much on offer at home yet with a slew of excellent personal reviews for his latest exploits, this seemed to be the moment for his Hollywood début.

It came in the form of a biopic, the life story (somewhat highly coloured) of the already flamboyant composer-pianist Franz Liszt. It was his first meeting with the French model Capucine, the only woman he ever wanted to marry and with whom he was to form a close attachment for the rest of her life. *Song without End* was a multimillion-dollar production lavishly built around Capucine by Charles Feldman, a Hollywood producer who had spotted her in a Paris restaurant when she was a top fashion model for giants like Chanel and Givenchy and had sent her a note suggesting that she telephone him if she ever wanted to be in films. When she got to Hollywood she moved into Feldman's mansion and he patiently groomed her to be 'the next Garbo, the next Bergman' for three long but happy years.

When Charley Feldman finally deemed her ready he invited Dirk to be her leading man partly because he didn't want squads of Hollywood leading men

PLAYING THE PIANO AFTER WEEKS OF FINGER-BLEEDING PRACTICE, DIRK AS FRANZ LISZT IN *SONG WITHOUT END* (1960). 'A FIASCO' (DIRK BOGARDE).

sniffing around his prize. Dirk jumped at the offer, at least until, in his first-class cabin on the *Mauritania* on the way to America, he read the script. Had he been able to turn the ocean liner around would certainly have gone straight back to Southampton. 'How, in God's name,' he moaned to Tony Forwood, 'can I ever say these terrible words?' 'With total conviction,' replied the ever-practical Forwood, unimpressed by Dirk's despair and somewhat amused to discover that Dirk would have to learn some of the most fiendishly difficult music in the classical repertoire in order to be convincing as the greatest pianistic virtuoso of his time.

What happened next was totally unexpected. Over the long and tedious shoot, after one director (Charles Vidor) actually dropped dead and another (George Cukor) made

WITH CAPUCINE, HIS CO-STAR AND THE ONLY WOMAN HE EVER REALLY WANTED TO MARRY, GREETING THE DIRECTOR GEORGE CUKOR WHO HAD FLOWN IN TO RETRIEVE *SONG WITHOUT END* AFTER THE SUDDEN DEATH OF ITS FIRST DIRECTOR, CHARLES VIDOR.

what sense he could out of the almost comically dreadful screenplay ('Pray for me, Mother'), Dirk found himself falling more and more in love with the beautiful Capucine, who was, however, firmly and permanently devoted to Feldman. The agonies of unrequited love were matched only by the equal torment of discovering that he had chosen a turkey for his all-important Hollywood starring début, not least because, as quickly became apparent, Capucine couldn't act at all. She played the Russian Princess to whom Liszt dedicated his 'Liebesträume', who divested herself of her husband only to discover that the Pope would not allow their marriage.

They were not to be the only agonies to be suffered on *Song without End*. The excitable Hungarian director Charles Vidor had had his heart attack not a moment too soon. He had taken to shaking an increasingly wooden Capucine until her teeth chattered, screaming at her, in a combination of Hungarian and Hollywoodese, 'Relax, *Reeeelax*', which, not surprisingly, had the opposite effect from that intended.

His heart attack took place while in a compromising situation with a young actress, who then had to be smuggled out of his room while his corpse was unceremoniously removed in a laundry basket 'to avoid scandal'. The KLM plane carrying his coffin (no other airline would transport a dead body during the tourist season) actually crossed at Vienna Airport with the one bringing George Cukor to the rescue.

The American
director had agreed to
take it over only on
condition of total
anonymity and,
although the idea of a
life of Liszt had been
around Hollywood
for sixteen years, ever
since Cornel Wilde
had scored an
amazing hit as
Chopin (*A Song to
Remember*), there was
now evidence that the
public's fascination
with lives of the great
composers was
waning fast. At just about the time they
were starting on Liszt, Alan Badel had a
disaster with the life of Wagner, a composer
much admired by Liszt (a sub plot of *Song
without End*).

On his arrival Cukor found himself
facing an idiotic script, dull sets, costumes
and furniture whose awfulness he could not
believe, an inflexible cameraman (James
Wong Howe), who had to be fired in favour
of one more compatible (Charles Lang).
Walter Bernstein was brought in to
drastically rewrite the most awful scenes,
and he and Cukor removed some of the
screenplay's worst dialogue — 'Hi, Franz,
seen anything of Schubert?' and 'Is that
Chopin over there by the door?' Even so,
the film proved irretrievable.

Song without End rapidly became a
collector's piece, not least for the scene

where Liszt, Chopin and
George Sand wander
through the streets of
Vienna singing 'Sur le
Pont d'Avignon' for all the
world as though they were
auditioning for a remake
of *Singin' in the Rain*.
Reviews were, on the
whole, fairly appalling. In
the view of Clancy Sigal, 'Dirk Bogarde
plays Franz Liszt with a heavy-lidded
petulance utterly in keeping with the
magnificent banality of the script; we have
not seen this kind of random eyebrow-
raising and facial twitching (designed I
suppose to convey creative neurosis) since
Miss Jennifer Jones' last picture.' For the
Daily Telegraph, Eric Shorter worried that
Dirk's Liszt looked far younger at the end

'BY THE END OF THIS ETERNAL
SONG, BOGARDE MANAGES TO
LOOK EVEN YOUNGER, HAVING
RETIRED TO A MONASTERY
WHERE, THE PRESS KIT TELLS
US, HIS FACE IS REFLECTING
THE INNER PEACE HE HAS AT
LAST FOUND.' CAPUCINE HERE
SEEMS TO HAVE FOUND IT TOO –
UNLESS OF COURSE SHE'S
ACTUALLY ASLEEP, AS WERE
MANY OF THE AUDIENCE.

of the picture when he retires to a monastery than he ever did at the beginning of his career. I suppose a less charitable critic might have assumed that Dirk's suddenly youthful appearance was in fact relief at having finally got through a film without end. In Britain the film was perhaps not helped by posters reading 'At Last — The Story of Liszt's Life with Dirk Bogarde'.

The only element of the film that garnered positive press was the soundtrack, which was played by someone never even seen on the screen. The piano sounds came from the brilliant South American concert pianist Jorge Bolet but the hands on screen belong to Dirk, who toiled long and hard in his piano studies until his fingers bled. Jorge Bolet was accompanied by the entire Los Angeles Symphony Orchestra. Every critic mentioned them, including several who paid tribute to the hours Dirk had put in in order to 'duplicate magically the actual playing'.

Dirk can be hilariously self-deprecating when he writes about his disasters. He was, about this one, his own best critic. Who else but the unfortunate performer himself would ever have dared describe his Liszt as having the appearance of 'a mad rocking horse in a pink candyfloss wig'?

There wasn't really time to take in the scale of the disaster because, although Capucine had made her preference for Charley

manifest by bringing him, uninvited, to a family Christmas *chez* Dirk, he still had hopes that she would relent and marry him. On arrival, Feldman sussed the depth of Dirk's feeling for her and, with considerable grace and good sense, had him quickly snapped up by another disastrous epic before he had time to remove Franz Liszt's Technicolor make-up. He was shipped to Rome to co-star with Ava Gardner and Vittorio de Sica in a Spanish Civil War epic in a role originally intended for Montgomery Clift. When Clift failed his insurance medical examination Charley saw an opportunity to get Bogarde out of Capucine's eyeline and out of harm's way and, with a few strategic telephone calls, arranged for Dirk to be summoned.

The film was *The Angel Wore Red* and Dirk

WITH AVA GARDNER AND THE FAMOUS HOLLYWOOD HAIRDRESSER SIDNEY GUILLAROFF ON THE SET OF *THE ANGEL WORE RED*. 'I JUST HOPED,' SAID DIRK, 'THAT WE COULD BANK THE MONEY AND QUIETLY FORGET IT EVER HAPPENED.'

was the unfrocked young priest falling in love with a cabaret entertainer against a background of the Spanish Civil War. His judgement was of yet another film and another star ruined by Hollywood. 'This was,' he told the *Evening Standard*, 'a magnificent part for Ava and it would have done for her what *Two Women* did for Sophia Loren. She really put her heart into it. I think she was anxious now to be more selective and make better pictures. So she played it without makeup, without a bra, and with holes torn in her dress. Then the word came from Hollywood. This wouldn't do. They wanted the old, glamorous Ava. So they put a corset on her and tidied her up. The life went out of Ava after that.' Most critics agreed with his assessment and blamed the director rather than the actors. 'The abounding impression of gloomy incompetence is reinforced by the deep involvement of Nunnally Johnson who both wrote and directed it.' Dirk was open about his lack of interest in the entire operation: 'I was just hoping to bank the money and forget the film ever happened ...

IN *THE ANGEL WORE RED* (1961) AS YET ANOTHER LAPSED PRIEST, THIS TIME CAUGHT UP IN THE SPANISH CIVIL WAR.

Larking around as a fallen priest with Ava Gardner is all very well when you are still a young man. But when you are turning forty you do want to do slightly more serious things.' Hollywood the place and Hollywood the industry never suited Dirk at all and although he did go back it was always reluctantly and rarely.

It was with a certain relief, then, that he came home to Buckinghamshire and the last couple of years still outstanding at Rank. But with the arrival of the sixties' social-realism films, Bogarde knew his number was up at home too. 'The Beatles and the King's Road were happening, Finney and O'Toole had come along, and I knew I'd worn myself out over here. The only good mainstream British films that I got now were ones for which they really wanted William Holden or Gregory Peck.'

Rank wasted no time in throwing him into a role originally designed for the ever-elusive Marlon Brando. This was the bandit Anacleto in *The Singer Not the Song*, reckoned

BACK HOME AT AMERSHAM, TRYING TO AGE GRACEFULLY INTO SOME RATHER BETTER SCRIPTS.

by many critics to be the first gay Mexican western, although you had to look very carefully to see that. Dirk, swathed entirely in black, was the villain who hates the church but loves its priest. The priest was played by John Mills, who seemed to think he was in a quite different film. Badly directed and inadequately edited, the picture gained its gay following partly on account of Dirk's tight black leather trousers and mainly from the final shot, which has the bandit and the priest both dying but locked in an embrace

AVA GARDNER VISITING DIRK ON THE SET OF YET ANOTHER OF HIS BLACK-LEATHER JOBS, *THE SINGER NOT THE SONG*.

TOP: ON LOCATION FOR *THE SINGER NOT THE SONG* WITH JOHN MILLS AND THE DIRECTOR/PRODUCER ROY BAKER. DIRK SAID, 'I PLAYED THE BANDIT LIKE GLORIA SWANSON IN *QUEEN KELLY,* WHICH AT LEAST GAVE ME A LAUGH.'

ABOVE: DIRK AND JOHN MILLS UNITED IN DEATH AS THEY NEVER WERE EARLIER IN THE PICTURE.

ABOVE: ON LOCATION READING
HIS REVIEWS FOR *VICTIM*
(1961), THE FIRST MAINSTREAM
FILM EVER TO TREAT HOMO-
SEXUALITY SYMPATHETICALLY
AND IN DETAIL.
OPPOSITE: 'A CAREFUL
PERFORMANCE BY BOGARDE
WHICH PURSUES WITH ELEGANCE
AND CONVICTION THE CASE
AGAINST AN ANTIQUATED LEGAL
STATUTE' (*TIME*).

as the bandit squeezes the priest's hand and murmurs, 'The singer not the song.' Dirk himself noted that he had modelled his performance on Gloria Swanson as *Queen Kelly*.

But if the homosexual undertones of *The Singer Not the Song* were in a kind of code, Dirk in his next picture became the first British star ever to take part in a mainstream film specifically about homosexuality. '*Victim* may shock my nice young *Doctor in the House* public, but you can't go on making films just to please your fans. You can't leave all the adult films to the French, Italians and Swedes.' Directed by Basil Dearden, *Victim* was the story of a respectably married barrister who risks his career and marriage to defeat an extortion racket when his former boyfriend commits suicide rather than identify him. In one sense this was just a routine blackmail

thriller with the added *frisson* of the love that dare not speak its name, but in a wider sense it followed the Wolfenden Report of four years earlier in demanding a change in the law of consent. At the time, 1961, nine out of ten blackmail victims in Britain were covering up their homosexuality at enormous personal and economic cost. What *Victim* said was that any law sending homosexuals to prison was bound to be a charter for blackmail, and that what consenting adults did in private was their own business. When the law was eventually changed, the makers of *Victim* and Bogarde himself could take at least some of the credit. 'It was one of the happiest films I've ever made. Many years later, when Lord Arran was fighting to have the Wolfenden Report passed by Parliament and by then I was living abroad, I got the most wonderful letter from him. He'd seen *Victim* on television, he'd never seen it before, he saw a late-night viewing of it and he made a lot of people come and watch it — he'd got a video, and he wrote and I still have and treasure his letter. He wrote to me in France: "Dear Mr Bogarde, You and I together have, with your film 'Victim', helped to change the law." So that was an achievement.'

Nearly forty years later it is hard for us to appreciate the courage that was required for a sex symbol like Dirk to agree to play what we would today describe as a bisexual, but Rank was also brave to be willing to put *Victim* on the major Rank-Odeon circuit. Some indication of what they were up against can be gleaned from a

review in *Time* which complained, 'Nowhere does the film suggest that homosexuality is a serious but often curable neurosis that attacks the biological basis of life itself. The picture at its most offensive is full of sodomites and, what is most offensive, an implicit approval of homosexuality as a practice.' The American censor actually refused *Victim* any seal of approval on the grounds that it was 'thematically objectionable' and it was therefore not shown except in art houses, where a special licence had to be sought.

Seen now, *Victim* is really a very cautious barricade-breaker; it was Dirk alone who insisted on strengthening the script by inserting a scene, which he wrote, between the barrister and his wife, admitting his desire for the boy and thus making it more dangerous for himself. A great many actors had already turned down the script, even though the word 'homosexuality' is never used and the film steps carefully around many of the issues involved. 'But I had

much more mail than I'd ever got and it was simply saying, "Thank you" and women wrote and said, "Now we know what was wrong" with their son or their husband or whatever it was. People had been living in shadows for years, not knowing what this cataclysmic thing that happened to their marriage or boyfriend or, even, girlfriend. So, in a way, I got the message that then I could use the cinema for valuable reasons as well as entertaining.'

For Dirk, the film was a mixed blessing. On the up side, his reviews were very good and he had finally achieved his ambition to make a film that would entertain but also would 'disturb and alert and cause people to question and worry'. On the down side, he had with one single picture seriously alienated his heartland *Doctor in the House* audience; he was to make many more good films at home and abroad but never again to top any box-office charts. *Victim* turned him overnight from a handsome action-adventure hero to a character actor working in a very different and much more risky genre.

Dirk's own view was, despite the down side, typically independent. *Victim* was, for him, 'the wisest decision I made in my entire cinematic life but it wasn't easy. We were all called together on the first day and given a talk that there were certain words not to be mentioned on the set — pansy, poof, that sort of thing. As the only homosexual on the film was lovely Dennis Price, we were all a bit bemused. I was away when the film opened. When I got back everyone said, "How brave." That

side of it never occurred to me. But I did get a lot of letters.'

And there was another problem: because the film was still treading very cautiously around its central issue, it never showed Dirk in any kind of homosexual encounter. This surely created considerable confusion, for the fatal graffiti scrawled across his garage door, accusing him of being 'queer', was in the North of England simply understood to mean that he had been feeling a bit poorly.

In a sense he had grown up at last and it was no coincidence that immediately after *Victim* he reached an amicable settlement with the Rank Organisation which released him from the rest of his contract. He was about to start on the much more dangerous, more exciting, more frightening, but vastly less profitable life of the freelance actor, a life which was to give him his best roles and, along the way, a good deal of heartache.

'AS THE SUCCESSFUL BARRISTER WHO MUST CONFESS HIS OWN HOMOSEXUALITY IF HE IS TO TRAP THE BLACKMAILERS, BOGARDE GIVES THE COMMANDING PERFORMANCE ONE HAS LONG EXPECTED FROM HIM' (*SUNDAY TIMES*).

ON THE
THRESHOLD

'Being with Garland,

working with her,

loving her as I did,

had made me the most

privileged of men.'

To start his new freelance career, Dirk decided to play safe. His last four films had all been box-office disappointments and he reckoned that a Napoleonic naval saga, *HMS Defiant* (*Damn the Defiant* in America), would at least get him back into the mainstream even if it did mean taking second billing to Alec Guinness. He played the mutinous lieutenant trying to wrest power from a gallant captain and, said the *Daily Express* gleefully, 'Bogarde has stolen the plum part in the film right from under Guinness's normally sensitive nose [as the] blood-happy villain who just likes to be surrounded by as much torment as possible.' Once again Bogarde had fallen right back into his previous British pattern of receiving personal plaudits for mediocre films and on this occasion the film was apparently so instantly forgettable that neither of Bogarde's co-stars, Guinness and Anthony Quayle, even refers to it in their own autobiographies. Dirk's memories were of his lieutenant being constantly beastly to his seafarers, while Sir Alec 'slapped his thigh from time to time in a grey wig which looked remarkably like a tea cosy'.

Nor was *HMS Defiant* helped at the box office by the fact that its release in 1962 coincided with that of Peter Ustinov's *Billy Budd* and the Brando remake of *Mutiny on the Bounty*. How many billowing sails and

OPPOSITE AND BELOW: WITH ALEC GUINNESS BEFORE THE MAST OF *HMS DEFIANT* (1962). 'BOGARDE STEALS THE FILM FROM UNDER SIR ALEC'S NORMALLY SENSITIVE NOSE BY PLAYING THE BLOOD-HAPPY VILLAIN WHO JUST LIKES TO BE SURROUNDED BY AS MUCH TORMENT AS POSSIBLE' (*SUNDAY EXPRESS*).

THE PASSWORD IS COURAGE (1962). 'DIRK BOGARDE'S COCKNEY HERO IS ADEQUATE ENOUGH UNTIL HE GETS THE IMPOSSIBLE TASK OF COMMENTING ON GLIMPSES OF AUSCHWITZ' (FINANCIAL TIMES).

dastardly officers could Odeon audiences cope with in a single year? Still, the film did buy Dirk and Forwood a little time in which to move from the Beaconsfield country house to a farm in deepest Sussex, which, being less expensive, would also give them some reassuring money in the bank now that the Rank cheques were no longer arriving monthly.

Dirk badly wanted next to do a screen adaptation of John Osborne's first play *Epitaph for George Dillon*, about a young actor-dramatist up against suburban respectability. Having the courage of his own admiration for Osborne, he had bought the film rights, but when no

producer showed the slightest interest he went back reluctantly to a routine Second World War drama, *The Password Is Courage*, which, set in prisoner-of-war camps, must have brought back some unpleasant memories of his own war.

Neither Dirk nor Forwood seemed to have a clear idea of just what they wanted from their new-found freedom from Rank, nor which direction they wanted to go in, other than a vague desire to make better films. Some indication that Dirk's career was now floundering was his decision to 'guest-star' as Dr Simon Sparrow in yet another seagoing farce, *We Joined the Navy*. Now, it was Kenneth More's film and his name alone above the title; nor was Dirk best pleased to discover that whereas in all his years as a contract artist the most he was earning was £12,000 a film, Kenny More, as a freelance, was on £50,000. Dirk's rather ghostly appearance as Sparrow (amazingly, he still had one more of his own *Doctor* films to make) suggested that, eager as he was to rebuild his career in more challenging and even dangerous scripts, he still liked to keep a toehold on the old Rank comedies that had once given him the commercial stardom he was never to find again.

While trying to decide what to do next Dirk was approached by his old friends Basil Dearden and Michael Relph, who had made *Victim* with him, to star in a futuristic thriller as an Oxford physiologist taking part in a water-tank experiment in which he is deprived of sight, smell, sound, touch and taste for eight hours in order to discover whether this could be a fiendish new way of brainwashing. *The Mind Benders* was respectably reviewed but again did very little at the box office for a public who were still having trouble coming to terms with the new 'experimental' Dirk.

His next film was essentially an act of pure charity. On his first trip to America, to discuss the possibility of *Gigi*, he had struck up a friendship with Judy Garland and, like so many of her friends, been turned into a mixture of psychiatrist and male nurse to this most neurotic of stars. On one of her many weekend visits to Dirk's country house, she took him a script by Mayo Simon and Robert Dozier. This was the story of an American singing star visiting London to top the bill at the Palladium who meets up with her first love, a British surgeon who then has to get her through nervous breakdowns and alcoholic fits on to the Palladium stage where, alone, she can find some kind of happiness. Obviously, this was a kind of closet biography of Garland, although she told him that she herself was never happy on stage but only after the curtain came down at the end of the performance. 'Working with someone like Judy Garland, who was basically a concert performer ... She was fit for tying every day of her life with terror before a show and the only moment that she felt good, I know, was when

the curtain finally came down, and I used one of her lines, that she used to me, in a scene I wrote for her once, when she says, "You know when the light hits you, the pain and the fear goes. It's a goddamn lie. It doesn't ... and it doesn't."'

Dirk was convinced that Hollywood had been the death of some of the screen's most important actresses. 'I mean, somebody as magical as Marilyn Monroe. Marilyn was totally and utterly murdered by them, by their system and, to a degree, Judy, whom I knew very, very well and closely for about ten years. I did her last movie with her but they killed Judy. They've killed anybody of any sensitivity. People said how brave I was to be in a film with

THE MIND BENDERS (1963). 'GREAT IDEA, BUT WHAT TO DO WITH IT? DIRK BOGARDE IN THE LEADING ROLE SEEMS A COILED JITTERY MAN TO BE PLACED IN A TOP SECRET LABORATORY' (*NEW YORK TIMES*).

OFF THE SET OF *I COULD GO ON SINGING.*

Judy Garland. I wasn't brave, I wasn't self-sacrificing. I wrote all her material and one of the greatest privileges of my acting life was to work with that actress. And she was a monster, she was monstrous, but she was magic.'

Dirk, aware of the film's limitations, but believing that it might still prove his beloved Judy's only real chance at a movie comeback, added a brilliant scene pinpointing Garland's own wayward nature. 'You think you can make me sing? You can get me there, but can you make me sing? I sing for myself. I sing what I want to, whenever I want to — just for me. I sing for my own pleasure. I'll do whatever I damn well want. You understand that?'

But once shooting started on *I Could Go on Singing* (originally, and rather better, titled *The Lonely Stage*) there were all the usual Garland drink and drugs problems. She behaved appallingly on the set, some days failing to show up at all, and wasting a good deal of her energy in trying to get the director, Ronald Neame, fired. Dirk behaved immaculately throughout, not only turning in the most self-effacing of performances but begging, bullying, nursing and cajoling Garland through every scene. Sadly, he was contracted to start another picture in seven weeks' time and as soon as he left the Garland set she fell to pieces once again, leaving Neame to try to put together both his star and the movie.

The film opened in both Britain and America to generally very respectful reviews, though Dirk's sacrifice of his own

role was noted by Paul Dehn: 'Bogarde, cast as Garland's former lover, has a role which seems to have been devalued somewhere along the line, reducing the character almost to that of a straight man cueing in his co-star to her complex of emotions. This Bogarde does with an unfailing unobtrusive tact, but his is not a role of much content.' And, as soon as the film opened, the producers made a horrific discovery.

Although Garland fans were still queuing around the block both at the Palladium in London and at Radio City in New York to see their idol live and maybe share in the macabre pleasure of witnessing her collapse on stage, they were no longer interested in seeing her on film. Although Garland could have gone on singing, her fans didn't want

WITH JUDY GARLAND, DIRECTOR
RONALD NEAME AND OTHERS ON THE
SET OF HER LAST MOVIE, *I COULD
GO ON SINGING* (1963). THE
TROUBLE WAS THAT SHE COULDN'T,
DESPITE LOVING COACHING AND
CONSIDERABLE SCRIPT-REWRITING
BY DIRK HIMSELF.

to hear her, at least on celluloid, which is a pity because, thanks to Dirk, *I Could Go on Singing* was not only her very last film; it actually contained a more truthful picture of her and her tortured life than any other. Even so, it died a rapid death, and Dirk had the humiliation of seeing its posters taken down after three days at his local cinema, where it was replaced by a revival of *Genevieve*.

Bogarde was now the gloomy sentry, forever waiting to be insulted by another inane script thudding through his letterbox. Too broody, too arrogant, too distant, too talented and too subtle ever to be taken to the mainstream of the film industry here or in Hollywood, he was so far from ever being gruntled that, starting from now, a wary, weary, elegant disgruntlement became a way of life and the source of his chronic internal exile.

He was, although he didn't know it, on the brink of a new and dangerously exciting

career in films. The last gasp of the old life was his fifth and last appearance as Dr Simon Sparrow, almost as though he were still determined to cling to the very last branch of his Rank stardom, having already cut down the rest of the tree.

Unfortunately, *Doctor in Distress* was just awful; the original inspiration of the Richard Gordon books had long since dried up and what was left was formula pap. It was Philip Oakes, writing in the *Sunday Telegraph*, who noted 'the sluggishness of the direction, the concealed advertising and the total waste of a talented cast who, in recognition of past pleasures, must remain nameless'. It wasn't even as though Simon Sparrow was his own exclusive property: Michael Craig had

BACK TO ST SWITHIN'S FOR THE
FOURTH AND LAST TIME. *DOCTOR
IN DISTRESS* CO-STARRED A
YOUNG SAMANTHA EGGAR:
'TOTAL WASTE OF A TALENTED
CAST WHO IN RECOGNITION OF
THEIR PAST ACHIEVEMENTS
MUST BE NAMELESS'
(*SUNDAY TELEGRAPH*).

starred in the last one. 'My trouble,' said Dirk at this time, 'is that I have never yet managed to be brilliant in a brilliant film. I've done some very good work in bad films, and been awful in some very good films, but those two excellences have hardly ever come together.'

But they were about to.

8 THREE EXILES

'Each of the four films

I made with Losey

between '62 and '66

was a bitter,

exhausting, desperate

battle.'

The idea of filming *The Servant*, Robin Maugham's novella about a master and a manservant effectively switching roles, had been around for a long time. Indeed, Joseph Losey had mentioned it to Dirk at the time they made *The Sleeping Tiger* back in 1954, and, quite independently, Harold Pinter had written a screen treatment for Michael Anderson. However, Peter Finch, the star Anderson wanted, wasn't keen to do it, and without him the budget of £250,000 proved impossible to raise.

Thus it was that Losey, acting on Bogarde's advice, managed to option the rights and slash the budget by half. Together and with a team, crew and growing company of other actors who were prepared to put 'career' second to values, they fought it on to film and then, when it was finished, off the shelf into the Warner Cinema in London. It was a tough haul for them all. None of the British distributors wanted it and none of the financiers was enthusiastic. But by now Losey had settled in London, the terrors of the McCarthy era were over and he was able with Dirk's help to push *The Servant* through the many layers of nay-saying that it faced.

Dirk recalls, 'It was the bitterest winter that year and after the first week of shooting, all on location, all in the cold, Joe called me and said, "I'm in hospital. I've got double pneumonia. They don't

OFF THE SET OF *THE SERVANT* WITH Jof LOSEY, THE DIRECTOR, WHO, MORE THAN ANY OTHER, HELPED DIRK TOWARDS SCREEN MATURITY.

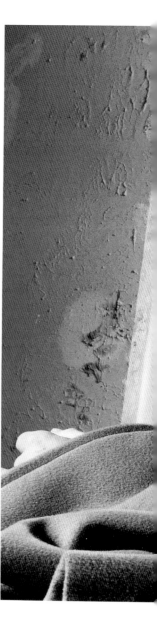

want to make the movie anyway, the Powers That Be. They'll 'can' it now — we're only a week in — and claim the insurance, unless ..." And I knew what he was going to say, and I said, "Joe, don't ask me to take over. I couldn't direct a bus." And he did and I did direct a bus. I directed and he directed through me from his hospital bed by telephone for the next ten days. So every take, every set-up, every lamp, every light — I was boss. The unit all called me "Mr Bogarde", nobody called me "Dirk". They paid me complete respect. It was wonderful. All my mates I've worked with for years

WITH SARAH MILES, HIS 'SISTER', ON THEIR WAY TO DESTROY THE LOUCHE LIFESTYLE OF JAMES FOX.

and everybody deferred to me. They knew I didn't know what I was doing, but they told me what I should be doing, so between them I got away with it, but it's my only scrape at directing and I'll never do it again — but we saved the film.'

Losey returned to finish his brilliantly sinister and secretive movie about power games and class distinctions and suppressed sexuality. With Dirk were Sarah Miles and James Fox (like Dirk, in some of the very best performances they ever gave) as the other two corners of a symbiotic triangle of unease and hedonism, rarely if ever filmed before. Losey thought them all brilliant but did not endear himself to one of the film's other stars, Wendy Craig, by announcing publicly that she had been badly miscast as the young aristocrat's even more aristocratic fiancée.

The Servant was first shown at the Venice Film Festival in September 1963, where it met a lukewarm reception from Continental critics. Two weeks later it was shown at the New York Film Festival but still no distributor on either side of the Atlantic was displaying any interest. 'The

drama with that movie was that nobody wanted to run it. Everybody said, "No, it won't work", "Who wants it?", "It's a nasty, ugly story", "It isn't entertaining, it's black, it's all about LSD at the end." It was partly owned by Warners, who were responsible for distribution, so they just put it in the cellar, where it remained for a long, long time. Until Arthur Abalees, the

European representative for Warner Bros here in London, had a week to fill at the Warner Cinema and he was going through a whole lot of stuff that was backlogged and one of them was *The Servant* and he said, "We've got to have this," and we had a première

THE MASTER AND THE MANSERVANT REVERSE ROLES: 'BOGARDE, RELISHING THE MOST SUBSTANTIAL ROLE OF HIS CAREER, ASSUMES A TEA-PARTY FAÇADE THROUGH WHICH THE GLEAM OF HELLFIRE IS ALWAYS DIMLY PERCEIVED' (*TIME*).

and we got reviews such as you've never seen before in your life, and we were off. But if it hadn't been for Arthur ...

'Joe and I thought, after *The Servant*, we were credible, both in America and here. I got back my box-office status and he was accepted in America: first time since the McCarthy thing he was allowed to go back to America and had outriders behind him because all his chums had been in the Mafia and this great Mafia gang took him in from the airport. It was terribly exciting. Bringing him back to his own city.'

Dirk's performance as the slippery, supremely evil Barrett, won him, for the first time, a British Film Academy Award and might even have led to an Oscar had American audiences not found *The Servant* a little too dark and difficult for wide

popularity. But the reviews at home were ecstatic. The *Daily Telegraph* reckoned 'Bogarde has never done anything better; a wonderfully macabre suggestion of a brutal nature beneath a smooth surface', while the critic Tom Milne believed that 'all British films will now be described as pre-*Servant* or post-*Servant*', so drastic did he believe its influence would prove to be. When the reviews came out, said Dirk, 'even Joe smiled. *That* was something.'

But there was still, even among all this new-found enthusiasm for Dirk and Joe, considerable confusion. The *Guardian* saw *The Servant* as 'the parable of a man and his alter ego'; the *Listener* thought it was 'a study of homosexuality'; the *Daily Telegraph* found it 'a film about possession, not merely who owns what, but who owns who'; while for *Time* it was 'an all out attack on Britain's class system'.

But the review that meant the most to Dirk came from Losey himself. 'Dirk fought the system and he carries scars, but I would say that he has won. In a sense he gave up stardom and security to become an actor who is always exceptional and frequently extraordinary. It is a pity the kind of world in which we must function still denies such talent continuity of work of the right kind it so palpably deserves and often withholds the rewards of appreciation when they are most needed.'

The real truth about *The Servant* is that it was the work of three exiles. Losey, exiled from his native America by McCarthy, Pinter, exiled from his East End roots by his West End success, and Dirk, exiled from mainstream British popular cinema by his desire to make thoughtful films.

For Pinter, a screenplay of pauses and menace was not so very different from his recent stage work in plays like *The Caretaker* and *The Homecoming*, but, of all critics, it was Alexander Walker who most intelligently understood that the timing could not have been better. 'By the time *The Servant* was premièred in mid-November, public reputations in Britain had come apart in the way that family heirlooms are traditionally supposed to do in the hands of careless domestic servants. This year, 1963, was the first year of rumours, doubts, suspicion and scandal about public figures ...*The Servant* managed to catch a state of change ... which British society already felt stirring and, because it was a work of art, it permeated one's cultural conscience more profoundly than any other film of the sixties. It exposed the arrogant, self-indulgent corruption of a privileged class dependent on exploiting an underclass whose civility is but a thin veil for long-standing resentments and desires.'

The Servant was a tremendous critical and art-house success but Dirk made no secret of the fact that if he was to make any more of these, and he urgently wanted to, he would have to finance them by diving back into the mainstream for commercial hits which could subsidize Losey's inevitably tight budgets. 'Dirk sometimes says he can't afford to work with me,' Losey commented wryly. 'Percentages and participations seldom get paid and our values and even those of audiences are not always the same as those of distributors and money. Eventually it becomes a question of which you put first. Dirk never gets them mixed up. He goes all the way for values or for money, but generally he doesn't confuse them.' So, once again, it was money's turn.

WITH ROBERT MORLEY IN AN ELEGANT ESPIONAGE COMEDY ORIGINALLY ENTITLED *008¹/₂* BUT WISELY RENAMED ON ITS FIRST RELEASE *HOT ENOUGH FOR JUNE*.

And Rank's: it was back to his old producer-director team of Betty Box and Ralph Thomas for a comic espionage thriller, hoping to catch the shirt tails of James Bond. Indeed, the film was originally entitled *008¹/₂* until somebody realized that was a little too close for copyright, and the picture was duly retitled *Hot Enough for June*. Dirk was the innocent spy and my father, Robert Morley, the treacherous spymaster in a perfectly amiable Bond spoof

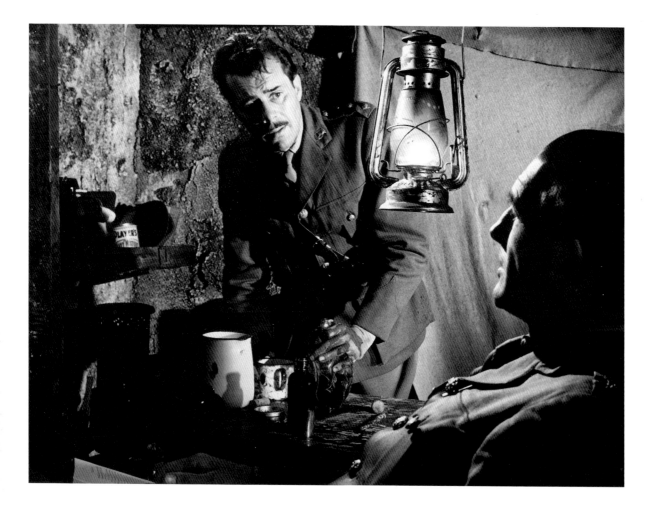

which many critics thought Dirk was doing 'as a rest from his better stuff'. It was true, of course, as Bogarde demonstrated immediately after by returning to Losey and the 'better stuff'.

What they came together for was *King and Country*. Set amid the rain and mud of the First World War's trenches, this was the story of a private soldier (Tom Courtenay) who has been struck by a fatal moment of sanity amid the madness of war so that he quite simply begins to walk home, away from the guns, only to be arrested for trial and execution as a deserter. Bogarde played the upper-class officer ordered to defend

him at the court martial who, at first reluctantly but then sympathetically, pleads the case of the common man caught up in unendurable horror. Losey said that Tom Courtenay's fine performance in *King and Country* would not have been possible without Dirk's generosity as an actor, and though Bogarde would never accept anything other than top billing he handed the film to the young Courtenay as a gift.

Losey was characteristically disparaging of the film industry establishment and

'DIRK BOGARDE BRILLIANT AS THE COLD OFFICER IN *KING AND COUNTRY* WHOSE SOUL IS SLOWLY WARMED INTO LIFE BY THE SIMPLE INNOCENCE OF TOM COURTENAY'S PRIVATE HAMP' (*SUN*).

unusually fulsome in his assessment of this movie. '*King and Country* was the best of both of us and yet although it cost only £85,000 it is still said to be in the red. It's on every TV screen all over the world constantly and yet

it is still "in the red". That kind of thing is hard on values.' Losey was referring to the now standard practice of giving directors and leading actors percentages or 'points' in a film's profits and then making sure, by various kinds of creative bookkeeping, that there are never any profits to share. Since

Losey's time there have been several spectacular court cases on this subject, usually resulting in modest pay-offs rather than wins for the actors.

In one sense *King and Country* had certain themes in common with *The Servant*. Again it was the work of outsiders, pointing up the corruption of the class system, whether social, military or religious; this is not just an anti-war film but another anti-establishment film of the kind that Bogarde and Losey were now doing best. For a boy whose family were rooted in the English and Dutch countryside, who had never known a day's poverty and whose entire military service was spent as an officer, Dirk had come a long way.

In the now familiar swing Dirk, the outsider, went back inside Rank to his film parents, Box and Thomas, for another formula war thriller. This one, *The High Bright Sun*, was set during the Cyprus unrest of 1957 and had nothing to recommend it except some sunshine and a good deal of Susan Strasberg as an improbable Cypriot-American who gets caught up in a really silly script by Ian Stuart Black. Dirk was intrepid as usual, doggedly doing his best but his heart wasn't in it. By now he'd been brilliant in a couple of really good films and he knew the difference. Said *The Times*, not unsympathetically, 'Before the beginning of his partnership with

Mr Joseph Losey, Mr Dirk Bogarde made rather a speciality of being splendid in appalling films. Here he is at it again; while on the screen, delivering Mr Ian Stuart Black's trite and improbable lines, our interest is aroused and we can even, by careful suspension of our critical faculties, believe one or two of them to be witty or intelligent. But really Mr Bogarde is battling against impossible odds.'

WITH CO-STAR SUSAN STRASBERG IN *THE HIGH BRIGHT SUN* (1965). 'BEFORE THE BEGINNING OF HIS PARTNERSHIP WITH LOSEY, BOGARDE MADE A SPECIALITY OF BEING SPLENDID IN APPALLING FILMS, AND HERE HE IS AT IT AGAIN' (*THE TIMES*).

9 EUROPE CALLING

'I am no longer box office but at least I'm distinguished.'

In 1965 came the film that was most emblematic of the sixties. *Darling*, starring the enigmatic Julie Christie, was the first popular film to point up the nihilism, the rootlessness, the form-over-substance glamour of its time. Christie's Diana is a model who persuades Dirk's character to leave his wife and children for her, only to tire of him and move on to fresher pastures elsewhere. John Schlesinger was the director. '*Darling* was really about choice,' he later reflected, 'about a girl who had the possibility of always thinking there was something better round the next corner, but was never capable of settling for anything, whether emotional stability or professional career ... I think it was very much a disease of the age.'

One of the central problems of the often brilliant screenplay by Frederic Raphael was the extent to which this was meant to be satire rather than a modern morality tale. Schlesinger himself later admitted, 'A lot of the things I thought were just funny in the film have somehow turned out to be ironic.' The Julie Christie character had somehow to be shown to be a bitch and yet keep our sympathy. Moreover, in capturing the compulsive promiscuity, professional and sexual, of the *Darling*

WITH DIRECTOR JOHN SCHLESINGER AND CO-STAR JULIE CHRISTIE ON LOCATION FOR *DARLING*.

ABOVE: LAURENCE HARVEY,
CHRISTIE, SCHLESINGER AND
BOGARDE DURING THE MAKING
OF *DARLING*.

LEFT AND RIGHT: WITH JULIE
CHRISTIE IN *DARLING*.

of the title, the apparent exploiter continually becomes herself the exploited party. Nobody quite knew where to put their sympathies for this caustic picture-essay on London, the kind that even now was starting to appear in the colour magazines. As for Dirk, he had not even been on the short list for the role of the television reporter who captures Diana's attention first. With an eye on the American market, the makers had first tried for Paul Newman or Cliff Robertson before 'settling' for Dirk. Schlesinger himself was later to call this his 'least good movie', adding, 'it simply hasn't stood the test of time'. But in fact, as a flashgun portrait of a moment in time, the moment of Swinging London, it serves still as a fascinating historical document. Coming in the age of *Private Eye* and BBC Television's *That Was the Week That Was*, the film could be viewed as a witty send-up of the Chelsea girls and the cover mannequins who were suddenly becoming stars. The characters, not least Julie Christie's beautiful but shallow Diana, were unsympathetic to an older audience accustomed to loving its heroes and heroines. The younger generation had no such scruples and they recognized *Darling* as a true picture of the kind of life many of them aspired to and believed was possible if they could only get to the Swinging

LEFT AND RIGHT: OFF THE SET AND DOWN THE UNDERGROUND WITH JULIE CHRISTIE IN *DARLING*.

London depicted in the film. Margaret Hinxman wrote, '... only Dirk Bogarde's performance touches a responsive chord, perhaps because he has the only halfway decent character to play, more probably because he has the experience and independence to create something true and moving from within himself.'

Dirk came off *Darling* on a high, knowing he had once again done really good work on a movie by a major director, and had received the plaudits. Although Julie Christie was the star, it was Dirk's participation in a supporting role which had anchored the movie and he knew it. He went back to Losey with the intention of turning all that good feeling into another good movie, this time one that added lightness to substance.

The thinking here was that Dirk and Joe now needed to prove that their work was not simply destined for art houses, and how better to plunge back into the mainstream than with *Modesty Blaise*, a famous *Evening Standard* strip cartoon, converted by Evan Jones

1965 AND THE START OF A NEW LIFE IN RADIO AS DIRK BEGINS THE FIRST OF MANY READINGS FOR THE BBC.

into a high-camp espionage romp? It may have once been a good idea but the execution was disastrous: the film seemed to suffer an identity crisis every twenty minutes or so and as usual Joe did not help matters by announcing as soon as the shooting was over that Monica Vitti in the title role had been badly miscast. Since he was the director and presumably in charge of casting, this repeated breast-beating is somewhat odd.

Dirk was deeply unhappy with his role (and especially his wig) as the arch-villain, and Terence Stamp complained that his part

WITH MONICA VITTI AND JULIE CHRISTIE AT THE LONDON PREMIÈRE OF *DARLING*, 16 SEPTEMBER 1965.

had been cut to shreds. For once Joe had been given a real budget of £600,000 but the money seems to have been frittered away on a series of ever more grandiose sets. His idea was to create here a 'toy for intellectuals' but there was no driving force to the plot and the anonymous critic of *Time* really went for it: 'Less a spoof than a limp-wristed kind of fairy-tale, utterly cluttered up with homosexual malice, artsy gift-shop decor and the same old gagging gadgetry on which the Bondmen have patents pending.'

A self-parodying actor like David Niven or Roger Moore might just have managed to make this one work; Dirk, never good at sending himself up, looked thoroughly uneasy wandering around drinking out of a wineglass that had a live goldfish swimming around the base. The image, like the film itself, was flashy and pointless. So much for Dirk and Joe's fantasy, although the director, while admitting Dirk's reservations, was still defiantly positive. 'Dirk

'DIRK DOMINATES THE FILM WITH A GLORIOUS PARODY OF A MASTER CRIMINAL WHO HATES SEX, EMPLOYS A COURT JESTER AND A MEDIEVAL FOOD TASTER, AS WELL AS A FEMALE EXECUTIONER AND A SCOTTISH PRESBYTERIAN ACCOUNTANT WHO CHIDES HIM FOR WASTING AMMUNITION' (*EVENING STANDARD*).

thinks we mixed things up. Perhaps to some extent we did (or, more accurately, *I* did) but I still believe that Dirk gave one of his best performances and demonstrated in that film a kind of icy wit which was new in his repertoire, though not in his character.'

But as usual it was Dirk who had the last word. 'Joe and I were still suspect because we weren't making films for general audiences. Nobody was going to queue up to see our work, which was too cerebral. *Modesty Blaise* failed because the two main artists [Monica Vitti and Terence Stamp] refused to play their parts as they should have been played, for high-camp comedy.'

It is a measure of the mutual respect and affection between Losey and Bogarde that even after the relative failure of *Modesty*

Blaise they should still have both been anxious to make their next film together, their fourth and, although they didn't know it at the time, their last and most commercially successful collaboration. *Accident* (1967) was based on the Nicholas Mosley novel, with a screenplay by Harold Pinter.

This is a fine insight into how closely

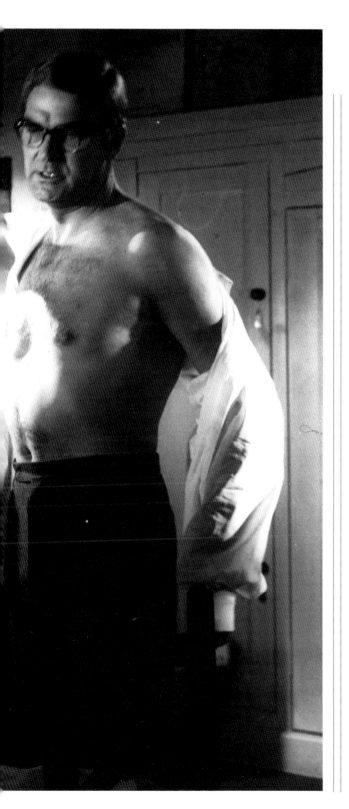

Bogarde enters the world of his characters. 'Stephen, the man I played in *Accident*, was a man I had never remotely been like, the antithesis of who I am as a person. It's much harder to play someone really so different to you, but physically so near you. Mentally, a totally different man, a don, married, two children, going through the menopause, which I don't think I have. I had to give him everything and he took over everything, and because it was Pinter you are following a railway line like a Hornby train set, you're not working and ad-libbing and chucking away lines. You've got to go through it, through the tunnels, through the little bridges, over the level crossings — everything as indicated.'

DIRK REUNITED WITH STANLEY BAKER FOR *ACCIDENT* (1967) WHICH ALSO BROUGHT BOGARDE BACK TO JOE LOSEY AND THE WRITER HAROLD PINTER. 'BOGARDE IS PREDICTABLY FAULTLESS AS HE WRITHES IN GUILT AND LUST WITHIN THE SKIN OF AN AVERAGE SENSUAL MAN' (*EVENING STANDARD*).

Accident consisted almost entirely of flashbacks and is about treachery, the way that people's acts betray their moral assumptions. It's also about apparently civilized men fighting over the same woman and, as Losey later explained, 'It's really about responsibility to other people, to what degree you indulge yourself at their

expense and to what degree you deny yourself and to what degree you can make your accommodations with them, without finding that you can't live with yourself.'

In a way this was a companion piece to *The Servant*. Instead of the closed world of a Chelsea house, we have the cloistered garden of an Oxford don, and this time Losey surrounded Dirk with an immensely strong cast: Stanley Baker as his rival at work and in love, Michael York as the young student with Vivien Merchant as his wife, betrayed in thought, word and deed but still in possession at fade-out.

For Michael York, the filming of *Accident* meant a kind of tutorial in screen acting from Dirk. 'He became my tutor in

ON THE *ACCIDENT* LOCATION WITH JOE LOSEY AND STANLEY BAKER. 'TWO OF THE BEST PERFORMANCES I HAVE EVER SEEN' (*GUARDIAN*).

more than just screen terms. He taught me about film acting, both by instruction and by example. His own method was a fine blend of intense concentration and instinct. Cinema, it has always seemed to me, is essentially filmed thought and you could almost hear Dirk thinking ... He also taught me other technical matters, especially about camera lenses and the importance of knowing which one was being used so that the performance could be adjusted accordingly ... Dirk also insisted on the supremacy of the script and how important it was to keep referring to it, not only at night, when one rehearsed the next day's dialogue, but constantly on the set.'

They both found it hard to let go when it was over. Dirk admitted later, 'I cried, I blubbed all the way home in the car from location when we finished *Accident*. I knew that Stephen had gone, but I was still manufacturing the person in my body. He was still around, I was still wearing his clothes, I was driving home but nobody wanted him and I had no need of him.'

By now the relationship between Dirk and Losey was showing signs of strain; Joe's confidence had returned in full measure and the combination of the terrible weather and the tight schedule began to tell on them both. Joe began to drink rather a lot, especially when there was a long wait for a set-up, and to take out his temper on the less senior staff. Dirk, who prided himself on his professionalism, hung in with him for most of the shooting until one two-a.m. shot when a well-oiled Joe yelled at him for having moved a prop, a child's bicycle,

WITH MICHAEL YORK IN THE FIGHT SCENE FROM *ACCIDENT*.

with the unfortunate phrase, 'Why can't you ever act professional?' Dirk, without a word, went to his car, drove back to London and didn't reappear for a week, by which time Joe had been on the telephone sobbing with apologies, begging Dirk to return.

Their relationship took a while to recover after that. They were a bit like an old married couple who had spent too much of a wet bank holiday in each other's company. They both needed a break. Dirk said later, 'We had used ourselves up. There was nothing more for us to say together; weary, drained almost, and to some extent disillusioned, we realized that we must separate for a time and go our own ways. After *Accident* I felt desolated, null, in limbo.' According to Dirk, it was Joe himself who said, 'Well, boyo, I think we'd better pack up together, because familiarity quite clearly is breeding contempt.' They never worked together again but their friendship and mutual respect lasted until Losey's death in 1984.

Dirk felt confident enough, for his next film, to ignore the theatrical stricture never to act with animals or children. Having enjoyed his experiences with little Jon Whiteley in *Hunted* and *The Spanish Gardener*, he launched into *Our Mother's House*, in which he was the only adult among *seven* children, with some

AS A SEEDY LITTLE COCKNEY CROOK IN *OUR MOTHER'S HOUSE* (1967), AT THE HEAD OF AN OTHERWISE ALMOST ALL-CHILD CAST.

enthusiasm. He played a no-good cockney cheeky chappie, who, after their mother's death, poses as their father, apparently in order to steal her savings.

Unfortunately, though the director was Jack Clayton, the script was appalling and the children appeared to come from all over the country, thereby displaying exactly the disparity of accents that proved they were not from the same family. Once again Dirk loved working with the children, and even though on screen his performance seems to lose heart about twenty minutes into the film, it was one of his happiest working experiences. Only after its lukewarm reception at the Venice Film Festival did it occur to Clayton and Dirk that it would not be a hit. Nobody there liked this movie, but it is chiefly remarkable for giving the adorable little Mark Lester his first chance at stardom. It didn't stick this time but the following year he was *Oliver* in the film version of Lionel Bart's musical and became, for a while, a big star.

Things didn't look up with the next film either. For *Sebastian*, a trendy spy thriller in which Dirk was an Oxford don doubling as a master code-breaker for John Gielgud as the Head of Intelligence, Dirk's reviews were respectful ('Bogarde now saves every picture he appears in') but Dirk realized that this was probably his last mainstream British starring role. Even the presence as co-star of his friend Lilli Palmer couldn't shake his conviction that his movie-star life had come to an end. He tended to agree with Ann Pacey, who wrote in the *Sun*, 'It is hard to understand what an actor like Dirk

WITH LILLI PALMER IN THE 1968 *SEBASTIAN*: 'BOGARDE IN HIS ELEMENT PLAYING THE THINKING MAN IN LOVE, AT WORK, AND AT WAR WITH HIS INTELLIGENCE CHIEFS' (*THE TIMES*).

Bogarde ... is doing in such a paralysing non-event as *Sebastian*.'

Dirk was bored with the scripts, with the roles, with the formula and, to a certain extent, with himself. He was coaxed by John Frankenheimer into a supporting role in *The Fixer*, an adaptation of Bernard Malamud's richly detailed novel about a Jewish odd-job man in Tsarist Russia. Alan Bates played the lead, with Dirk in the small but crucial role of the Government lawyer who alone believes in his innocence of the ritual murder of a Christian boy. 'There was really nothing for me to do here and invariably when I have too little to do, I always do too much, being under the impression that I have to do something to justify my salary,' Dirk says apologetically of his performance in *The Fixer*, a comment interesting for its insight into his Protestant work ethic. Never an actor to take the money and run, he has always done his best, even when the film or

the role didn't deserve him.

But now things had to change. Forwood and Dirk discovered, to their horror, that there was less than £8,000 in Dirk's account. Bogarde's description of that time is bleakly funny. 'The last two films I made in Great Britain were American-financed. Nineteen sixty-eight, that was curtains for me; Shepperton went, Pinewood went and the money went. So there was Uncle Dirk left with nothing to do and all these new children came whizzing in — the Tom Courtenays, the Albert Finneys, the Terence Stamps — rightly, because you have to have a recharge. But I did get an offer for a commercial which I'd always refused to do. They paid me £25,000 to run up and down the Spanish Steps in sunglasses.'

Without realizing it, Dirk had in those thirty seconds already made his début as a European film star. Among those who saw the commercial when it was shown in Rome was a director called Luchino Visconti.

AS THE GOVERNMENT LAWYER BIBIKOV IN JOHN FRANKENHEIMER'S *THE FIXER* (1969). 'IT IS BECOMING ALMOST A CRITICAL CLICHÉ TO PRAISE BOGARDE AS THE SAVIOUR OF SHAKY FILMS AND WHEN HE MEETS AN UNTIMELY END, THE FILM'S REINS SLACKEN, LEAVING US WITH NO CATHARSIS' (*SUNDAY TIMES*).

10 THE ULTIMATE TEST

'While I was in Rome Visconti sent me a script and asked if I'd like to work with him and that's really how The Damned *started.'*

The Damned was essentially *Macbeth* updated to the burning of the Reichstag in 1933. In a barely disguised portrait of the Krupps, it followed the fortunes of the Essenbeck steel family, examining the internal power struggles of a dynasty divided by the various members' attitudes towards the Nazis. As always with Visconti, the script had gone through various drafts and at least three titles, one of which was *Götterdämmerung*, suggesting an Armageddon and the heights of grand opera to which Visconti always aspired.

The film featured a massacre, arson, homosexuality, pederasty, sado-masochism, incest, madness, transvestism, patricide and matricide, with Bogarde as the outsider trying to claw his way to the top of the family firm, who were, by now, well in with the Nazis. By the time Dirk joined the cast, the film was already weeks behind schedule, a not unknown occurrence on a Visconti shoot, especially as the great director was in the habit of staying home on the days for which he thought he hadn't been paid. The budgetary process was the usual Italian shambles and Visconti got everyone and himself paid by the simple expedient of staying home when the money didn't arrive. This certainly helped *esprit de corps* but did nothing to keep the film on schedule. Dirk had been offered another Hollywood film just as he started *The Damned*, so he had the added pressure of working on an Italian-German-Swiss co-production in a foreign language, while trying to finish in time to get to Tunis for his next contracted project, the film of Lawrence Durrell's *Justine*.

His technique, one of the strongest in the business, stood him in

As Bruckmann in Visconti's 1969 picture *The Damned*: 'a lugubrious Englishman who keeps selling his soul over and over again to the devil' (*Sunday Times*).

ABOVE: THE DINNER-PARTY
SCENE FROM *THE DAMNED*,
DIRK CENTRE LEFT.
OPPOSITE: WITH VISCONTI
ON THE SET.

the best stead yet. In the famous dinner-party scene, where Dirk had a long monologue to make to a room entirely full of the Essenbecks and their cronies and retainers, the schedule broke down to the point where none of his co-stars was still on the picture. Dirk, always proud of his ability to act with white chalk marks, tells the story: 'I did the whole of the key scene in *The Damned*, in the studio with sixteen people at a dinner table and not one of them was present. But we had done the master shot and the actors couldn't get there for various reasons — fog, goodness knows what delays. There was no one on the set and Luchino was in despair and

said, "Wrap. We close now." And I said, "Look, I can do it. I know what the scene is about. Put the chalk marks at the eye levels, where all the people are"... There were two children but all the rest were adults but at different heights, so I had different eyelines to look at. I did the entire scene in one take. That is not swanking, that is what I am paid to do, but I could imagine them there. Because I'd seen them, I'd done the scene with them the day before. But this time it was to empty chairs, but it didn't throw me. Why should it? I was playing to the camera which was looking at me. It's great. Nothing could be more fun.'

Years later, talking to Barry Norman, Dirk recalled with some exasperation Visconti's penchant for taking huge bites

'I HAVE LONG ADMIRED MR
BOGARDE BUT I CANNOT SEE HIM
AS VISCONTI'S ANSWER TO
MACBETH' (DILYS POWELL).

'VISCONTI HAS PERHAPS SPENT
TOO MUCH OF HIS TIME
DIRECTING OPERA; WHAT WE
HAVE HERE IS STOLID, AND
STAGY' (DAILY MAIL).

out of the film during the editing process. 'I was bloody good in it, though you'd never know that from the English version. In England, it must have seemed like the first time an actor with his name above the title had played his entire role with his back to the camera.' Dirk's ego was still intact.

He managed to get away from Visconti in the nick of time to join the North African location of *Justine*, only to find that film already in deep trouble. The original director, Joseph Strick, was about to be fired in mid-shoot for a series of budgetary and personnel problems, and orders had come from the head office of Twentieth Century-Fox that the entire film was now to retreat to Hollywood, where a new director would be found.

The international cast included Anouk Aimee in the title role, Michael York as the poet who narrates the story, Dirk Bogarde as the exhausted British diplomat and Jean-Luc Godard's ex-wife, Anna Karina, as a belly dancer. Back in Hollywood, the replacement director turned out to be Dirk's old friend George Cukor, thereby giving Bogarde the unique distinction of having worked on two Cukor takeovers. But the problem of making over Lawrence Durrell's novel for Hollywood was considerable. The local by-laws forbade the use of real children for the children's brothel sequence, so

WITH GEORGE CUKOR AS SHOOTING BEGAN ON *JUSTINE* (1969).

several elderly dwarfs had to be hired for that and, as Dirk later remarked, most of the sets looked like the coffee shop of the Tunis Hilton while Hollywood's idea of Alexandria 'had all the mystery, allure, and sin of the roof garden at Derry & Toms'. Reviews were, predictably, very mixed, ranging from those who thought that Durrell's masterpiece had been totally butchered, to *The Times*, which noted, 'Bogarde sails through the muddles with an air of tired professionalism that suits the part admirably. All the others seem merely tired.'

By now Dirk and Forwood had decided that, for them, England was over. Dirk was now close to fifty, and the increasing economic problems, coupled with an awareness that a whole new generation of northern actors were taking the few roles Dirk might have wanted, convinced him that if there were any good offers they would come from Continental rather than British directors, who now saw him as a kind of relic from a previous generation.

Uncertain whether to settle in France or

OFF THE SET WITH MICHAEL YORK IN *JUSTINE*.

in Italy, they first took a year's lease on a villa in Rome and no sooner had they moved in than Visconti arrived for lunch, bringing with him a small present, neatly wrapped in ribbon. Dirk opened it to discover a paperback copy of *Death in Venice*. It was to be his greatest screen performance — but nothing is ever that easy. With only a quarter of the budget raised in Italy, Visconti turned to Hollywood financiers, who said they would be happy to back the movie but on just two little conditions: first, that Dirk be replaced with a bankable American star and secondly, that the boy, Tadzio, be turned into a girl, thereby removing the taint of homosexuality — and with it, of course, the whole point of the film. Visconti had also neglected one small detail: he had forgotten to clear the rights to the Thomas Mann novella itself (José Ferrer had bought them and demanded a considerable pay-off to release them) and by the time this was sorted out another three months had gone by.

Dirk always said later that being asked by Visconti to play Von Aschenbach was like having Larry Olivier invite you to play Hamlet, only much, much better. There's no doubt that if Bogarde is to be remembered for any one single performance, it has to be the 1971 Aschenbach. In all his subsequent writing, Dirk makes it clear that this was the defining moment of his career, the one for which he had essentially turned his back not only on Britain but also on the

ASCHENBACH ON THE LIDO: 'A BRAVE ATTEMPT, ALWAYS SENSITIVE TO THE ORIGINAL BUT FINALLY NOT QUITE THE SAME THING' (*MONTHLY FILM BULLETIN*).

DIRK CALLED IT 'THE BEST AND
MOST DIFFICULT ROLE I HAVE
EVER HAD TO PLAY'.
'CAMP AND MISCALCULATED
FROM START TO FINISH ... A
PRIME CONTENDER FOR THE
MOST OVERRATED FILM OF ALL
TIME' (*TIME OUT*)

whole of his previous life; this was also the film that has made his nine subsequent movies seem something of an anticlimax. It would be hard to think of any other actor, with the possible exception of Gielgud and Scofield, who could better have played the tortured composer at the end of his life, dying for the love of a golden boy whose very existence he can hardly bring himself to acknowledge. In reality, of course, Mann's story was based on Gustav Mahler and this gave Visconti the opportunity to set virtually the whole of the film to his greatest music. Again, it is Visconti's sense of the operatic that gives *Death in Venice* its ultimate power and,

although when they first showed it at the Venice Festival it was beaten to the prize by Losey's *The Go-Between*, there can be no doubt which film has better stood the test of time.

For Dirk it was the most testing role of his career. '*Death in Venice* practically did for me, because that was eight months and I was entirely alone. I had no one with me. I had to keep this wretched little Von Aschenbach, peevish fellow though he was, with me all day long. I never went to a lunch or anything and Visconti never asked me to. They all broke for lunch and went to the canteen. I had a tin of beer and a lightly boiled sole and I can't tell you how boring that is for eight months, but I couldn't eat anything. I was holding him. I know it sounds rather pretentious, but I really was. It's the only way I can work.'

The only instruction that Visconti ever gave him on *Death in Venice* was, one day, about two-thirds of the way through the shooting of the movie on the Grand Canal. 'It was noon, in the middle of lunch time, hot, hot sun overhead and I was in this tiny little motor boat going under the Rialto Bridge and he was in the boat beside me with the camera crew, they were shooting side on, and he shouted at me through a megaphone, "Bogarde! When you get under the bridge you feel shadow, uh? Then you stand, stand when you feel the sun." Then I felt the shade going over my head and then I saw the sun and I rose to the sun and that moment on the screen is the moment in Mahler when that great surge of that symphony comes roaring up and brought

the audience to its standing ovation, because I didn't know he was going to choreograph everything I did to the music of Mahler. That is why the musical tape, on record or compact disc of the film music, does not please professional musicians because the orchestra was orchestrating to my movements and if I was slow, then it was slow and all entirely due to me and I had no idea.

'I've never done a film that was anguishing beyond *Death in Venice*, which was a physical anguish in a desperate

endeavour to be something extraordinary, like a legend from modern literature. After all, our film set off a whole bloody opera and then a ballet, for God's sake. And, as Visconti said, when I put my glasses on and my moustache on, because I hadn't got anything else to put on — the nose that he'd made for Mahler didn't fit and filled up with sweat and fell off all the time, he said you can't use that, and we've got to shoot because of the insurance and I put on a moustache and a pair of glasses that Forwood had found in a cardboard box of jewellery, junk jewellery, in the wardrobe. And I put on the hat, put on the scarf and went down the stairs and I was Von Aschenbach — and the point is that after we'd finished the film, I said to Visconti, "Well, he's gone," and he said, "Yes, but no one will ever be able to do him again and if they do, they'll have to wear your clothes," and they have, because anybody wearing a white Panama hat and a white suit is Von Aschenbach, even if they're the size of a bus.'

Dirk was immensely grateful to his mercurial director. 'Visconti was the greatest teacher and professor I've ever had in my life. I've learned so much from him and from people like him and I was able to hand it on to other people. The fact that he and Losey and Cukor, and Schlesinger to a degree, never told me what to do. No one ever did that. None of my directors did. They would say what not to do.'

For Dirk privately, one of the great rewards for this performance was a telephone call from his father, Ulric, who had always taken rather a dim view of his elder son's career and refusal to follow him on to *The Times*. After seeing the film Ulric made a typically economical phone call: 'I just want you to know that I was very touched to see my father again, up there on the screen.'

For the filming, Visconti took over the Grand Hôtel des Bains on the Lido, a perfect period palace,

and Dirk spent the whole of the filming living in a kind of retreat as Von Aschenbach. Around the hotel Visconti meticulously built up a story of lost youth and forbidden love with Bjorn Andresen playing Tadzio, the golden boy in his sailor suit, forever leading Aschenbach towards a destiny at once known and unknown, until his inevitable death becomes the result not only of cholera and old age, but also of his lust for an unattainable perfect youth. 'In physical respects,' recalled Dirk, 'Bjorn Andresen was the perfect Tadzio. He had an almost mystic beauty. On the other hand, he had a healthy appetite for bubble gum, rock 'n' roll, fast motorbikes and the darting-eyed girls whom he met, tightly jeaned, ruby of lips, playing the pin-tables in the local Lido

WITH VISCONTI AND THE HAT.

LEFT: DIRK CALLS IT A DAY.
ABOVE: THE OLD MAN AND THE GOLDEN BOY.

hotel bar. The last thing he ever wanted, I am certain, was to be in movies ... he spoke fluent English but in the curiously mutilated manner of American disc jockeys, which was perfectly reasonable, since he spent most of his time listening to the American Forces Network. Thus his every other word was "hey", or "I dig" or "crazy" or, most often, "man". Fortunately, as Visconti told me drily, he was never required to open his mouth as Tadzio, so the enigmatic, mystic illusion which he appeared to have could be preserved.'

Silvana Mangano, swathed in Givenchy, was the boy's beautiful mother, a role coveted by Dirk's old friend Capucine, now alone since Charley Feldman's death and living in solitary luxury in Lausanne. She begged him to intercede with Visconti to cast her, pointing out that at least she, as a former model, would know how to wear the clothes, but although Dirk tried, Visconti wouldn't be budged. Later still, alone and convinced finally after forlornly going round the film festivals with a minder that there really was no future for her as an actress, Capucine committed suicide by jumping off the apartment building

THE DEATH OF ASCHENBACH.

underneath.' Her enthusiasm was shared by George Melly: 'For some reason there is still a tendency to treat this remarkably good actor rather patronizingly, to appear slightly surprised he can act at all. Perhaps this dates from his early days with Rank, but after his performance here I trust all doubts will be exorcized. It's a truly great performance in that every irritable word and old-maidish gesture adds to our knowledge of what is going on inside his head. If he doesn't win an Oscar, there's no justice.'

Feldman had bought for her. But all that was far into the future.

Death in Venice captured awards all over the world, though not the Oscar that Dirk so richly deserved. Margaret Hinxman, for the *Sunday Telegraph*, noted, 'There can be no doubt that Bogarde here gives the performance of his life, confirming his pre-eminence among screen actors: a portrayal of infinite detail which never lets the external cleverness of stance, gesture and makeup obscure the character deeply rooted

There was no justice, and in fact the most chilling comment on *Death in Venice* came from Dirk himself. 'For me, *Death in Venice* is the peak and the end of my career. Oh, I shall go on working to earn money, or if a project interests me, but I can never hope to give a better performance in a better film than *Death in Venice*. One critic ended his review with the words, "It is like the death of a friend." He understood.

'When I left *Death in Venice*, I remember taking off those spectacles that I had to wear, I had no makeup and I'd had my hair cut off because I'd grown it quite long and I hate long hair, and I watched the wardrobe lady wrapping everything up and putting it all away and that was Von Aschenbach. I had three suits and she wasn't hanging them on a hanger for tomorrow, they were being rolled into a bundle like for Oxfam. That was the end of him and his high button boots I saw slung in there and I thought "Good riddance" to those anyway. He'd gone, and like all love affairs that finish — they have to, intense, burning ones do — it's a form of desolation at the end, of course it is. And that's possibly partly why one behaves so stupidly. I mean, I cried for him.'

Dirk wept all the way home in the car because, as he said, he had kept this man with him for eight months and nobody wanted him any more, not even Dirk himself.

It was time for a new life and Dirk and Forwood found it, and the happiest twenty years of their lives, in a fifteenth-century farmhouse near Grasse, in Provence. There Dirk found a curious kind of freedom, privately to live the secluded country life he had always craved and

publicly to rethink not just his career but his life. It would still be a few years before he discovered the whole other world of the novelist and memoirist of some ten books which have so enchanted a quite different audience from the one that welcomed Dr Simon Sparrow to its heart. Professionally, he was also experiencing a kind of involuntary freedom. His last two Hollywood efforts — *Justine* and *The Fixer* — had been so far from triumphant that there were no more offers coming from there; nor did Dirk wish to receive any: 'There is a terrible fascination with Hollywood. It's like coming upon a street accident; you don't want to see all the blood but

AT HOME IN THE ONE PLACE HE FOUND TRUE HAPPINESS, HIS HOUSE IN FRANCE, LE PIGEONNIER.

GUEST-STARRING FOR RICHARD ATTENBOROUGH IN *OH! WHAT A LOVELY WAR* (1969).

you can't help yourself.'

Now all he was getting from Britain was what he described as 'the same old rubbish', so he felt free to take jobs that even five years earlier he would not have considered. As a favour to his old friend Richard Attenborough (now making his first film as director) he turned up as an effete aristocrat for one day's work on *Oh! What a Lovely War*. He then appeared, somewhat more bizarrely, as Bonnie Prince Charlie, in a thoroughly eccentric NBC television dramatized documentary about the history of the Basilica of St Peter's in Rome. Other casting for this collector's piece included Orson Welles as

Michelangelo, Ralph Richardson as King James II of Scotland and Dame Edith Evans, some way from Garbo, as Queen Christina of Sweden.

Still believing that his star career had now ended, he broke another lifelong rule by accepting third billing to Yul Brynner and Henry Fonda in a routine spy thriller for Henri Verneuil called *The Serpent*, which required him to be smooth and sinister as a Kim Philby-like double agent. As to why he was willing to accept the role on those billing terms, Dirk commented just after the shooting, 'Verneuil, whom I respect, was very persuasive and so was the money. I'm only in the film for about five minutes. But at least I was able to wear modern clothes and get away from the despicable label that the big film business boys had tied on me after *Death in Venice* — a fag actor! Besides, I had always worshipped Henry Fonda and naturally wanted to work with him; who wouldn't?'

But there was not enough meat in the role and Dirk fell back into his old habit of doing too much when there was too little to interest the technical actor in him. Russell Davies, in the *Observer*, noticed this immediately: 'Bogarde's first appearances in background and reaction shots are in his fractionally-raised-eyebrow style of acting which augurs not well and indeed he droops urbanely through his few scenes, shifting inside his suit, rolling his tongue from cheek to cheek and offering in short all the shrugs, pouts, and minute disclaimers that usually indicate he has been given nothing to occupy his mind.'

The film had started with some terrible news. A couple of days into the shooting Dirk's brother, Gareth, rang to say that Ulric had died suddenly of a heart attack. Dirk never quite forgave his mother for forgetting the doctor's telephone number and not calling him until an hour after Ulric's death. It was 1973, a time of transport strikes, and Dirk was allowed only twenty-four hours off the film to get to the funeral in England. He and his sister and brother were surprised and touched by how many of his father's friends and neighbours came to pay their respects. But Dirk was due back in Paris by the afternoon train. Mourning would have to wait.

When Dirk and Forwood moved into their beloved Le Pigeonnier the idea had been for Bogarde to move gracefully into a kind of rustic semi-retirement; but as it became clear how much had to be done to both the house and the surrounding land, Dirk found himself back in the old money trap. He had been paid only £50,000 for *Death in Venice* and that was soon eaten up by the new house. Several years later he was to tell the *Daily Express* that he had made *Death in Venice* 'for only £7,000'. Whichever it was, there was still nothing in the bank and at least once a year, until he turned into a more or less full-time writer,

he had to make a film for the exchequer.

In 1974 Dirk was offered the leading role in a film about a former Nazi who has chosen to live out his life in the half-world of a hotel at night. The script was by a young woman, Liliana Cavani, who, after seeing *The Servant* and *Darling*, had written it with Dirk in mind. Partly because of her youth and partly because he was not interested in the subject matter, Dirk turned it down. One evening, by accident, he watched a television film. 'I was

DIRK AND HENRY FONDA AS THE SPYMASTERS OF *THE SERPENT* (1974).

absolutely spellbound. It was the most wonderfully photographed film, rather like Losey used to do, and it was in the most incredible colour and wonderful costumes and God knows what. I couldn't understand much of it as I was watching sub-titles in French. However, I was interested enough to stay with it until the end, and I thought, "Wow! if this director ever asks me to act ..." and I waited and the titles came up. It was Liliana Cavani and a bell rang: "I've got a script from that woman ! It's down in the cellar" — that's where we keep the wine, the garden shed stuff, whatever — and down I went to the cellar and there, sure enough, was a thick tome, covered in blue mould and damp and

WITH CHARLOTTE RAMPLING IN LILIANA CAVANI'S 1974 FILM *THE NIGHT PORTER*.

beetles and I read it through again that night and it was about two o'clock in the morning when I finished, or three, and I called the next morning and accepted. So she came to see me and we worked on it together and we made *The Night Porter*. The script was enormous and was full of political polemic which I knew would not work as a movie, so I took out of it, with Liliana, that central story of a man in love with a lady and in a camp and what happened to them, that's all. Left and right of it we had to ditch. My only insistence was that Charlotte Rampling would be in it and because I chose not to take a salary, or a very little one, they gave me Charlotte Rampling, but they wanted to have a girl called Romy Schneider, who was a very, very popular and famous actress but I thought that was silly because she was German and though she spoke wonderful English and was adorable as a creature, she'd have been the Captain of the Guard and I would have been the prisoner. She's a very tough lady. As for Charlotte, she was only twenty-one and it was left to me to explain what had actually happened in Buchenwald and Auschwitz.

'There is a big scene

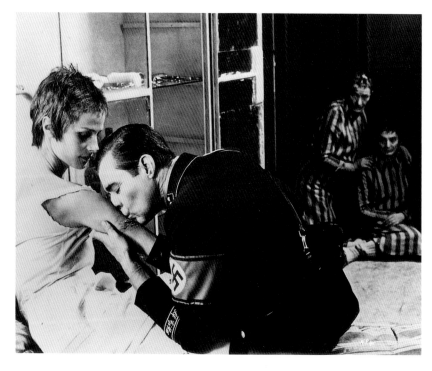

at the end of the film where Max is confronted by his fellow Nazis, who are all in hiding and have changed their way of life because they are now pretending they weren't Nazis, and we had a great big meeting on the roof of Stephansdom, the cathedral in the middle of Vienna, and the very morning we were going to shoot, that was the morning that they convicted Eichmann, and in the morning paper I took the entire defence speech from Eichmann and repeated it on the roof of the cathedral — that is exactly what Eichmann said, including, "I'm very proud of what I did for my country and if I was asked to do it again, I would." And that nobody believes, but it's in the archives, it's there. So Max indeed was a monster but the awful and terrible thing is — and I could talk to you a lot about fan-mail — but I got more fan-mail from that than I've got from any film ... from women who simply said, "One question ..." — nothing about the film or anything else, but: "Where can we find a Max?" So work that one out.'

The film was the story of the Nazi officer, now in hiding as a night porter, meeting again a woman he had seduced in a concentration camp. Dirk thinks of this as a love story rather than a film about ex-Nazis, but there were many who disagreed, finding it either a tedious art-house flop or a singularly unpleasant advertisement for sado-masochism as wounds were licked and co-star Charlotte Rampling was presented with the decapitated head of a prisoner who had once tormented her.

'The whole film just breathes disgust,'

'WHEN I WORK I WANT TO WORK WITH YOUNG EXCITING TALENTS' (DIRK BOGARDE).

thought Alexander Walker, and in America reviews were even worse. Pauline Kael wrote in the *New Yorker*, 'Bogarde is now just overexposed. We know all his neurasthenic tricks — the semaphoric eyebrows, the twitching mouth, the sneak vindictive gleam, the pinch of suffering are all warmed-over from earlier performances.'

Dirk's relish in the film's reception is almost gleeful. 'The Germans banned it. The Italians said it was disgusting, it was

obscene, and Charlotte and I and Liliana were on a summons for indecency if we ever set foot in Italy again. And it got really very, very, very hairy and gruesome but at one point I made a plea with Liliana, who knew "somebody" in authority, that "somebody" would see it. "Somebody", in inverted commas, in Italy, in Rome, and "somebody" did see it and said, "No. It's a masterpiece. It must be seen." It wasn't considered pornographic, so it was put on in Italy. It caused a huge sensation and there were nights and nights and nights of fighting queues and people ... Jews marched, saying it was against the Jews and the pro-Nazis marched and said it was against the Nazis, and there were battles all over the place. The Arabs got in on the act too and said it was against the Palestinians. I don't know, everything went wrong, but the film got shown.'

From Dirk's perspective his young director had found a new way of looking at the events of the century, although he was, even at the time, 'terrified it will get into the wrong hands and be released as a "sexploitation movie", which it totally isn't'. His

terror was justified. In America the film's distributors decided, in desperation, to try to market it as hard porn. For the press show critics were seated in black leather chairs with chains across them and given little matchbooks inscribed with whips.

By contrast, it was the freshness of Cavani's vision that Dirk loved, and the way she worked convinced him that 'in future, when I work, I want to work with young and exciting talent. All the same, this was a very strange experience for me. Some of the scenes in *Night Porter* — they *have* to be. And, in the middle of one, it would suddenly strike me: What on earth am I, that nice young Dr Simon Sparrow of the *Doctor* films, *doing* here?'

What he was doing was moving with the times,

living on the cutting edge, a trick he has always, mysteriously, managed, despite complaining bitterly about any kind of change. And technically, as experienced as Dirk was by this time, he was still practising his Alan Ladd lesson of 'the great look'. 'I think that's one of the perfect examples of a great look, it's the moment when Charlotte's character as a rich married lady, now living in America, comes back to the hotel and suddenly finds that the concierge behind the desk, the night porter, is the guy who was her guard at the camp and he's gone to ground and is a night porter. He isn't seen in the day — he only lives

DIRK GOES UNDERCOVER IN *PERMISSION TO KILL* (1975).

at night — and that look between the two of them is, I think, quite magical. And the look in the theatre, when they're both at the Opera in Vienna and he's behind and she knows he's behind and she turns and he's gone. Her building the terror and fear without any dialogue — it's all so good.'

Despite his many protestations that his major films were now in the past, Dirk was astute enough to realize that he still had to protect his image if he was ever again to work in the industry. As a result, he now went back, yet again, to a daft and often unfathomable espionage thriller, *Permission to Kill*, for the very simple reason that 'It got me out of that awful rut after *Death in Venice* and *Night Porter* when all the scripts I was offered featured ageing queers or perverts.' This, however, was not the script to perform that miracle, or indeed to do anything positive for him at all. As Philip French noted, 'The acting is uniformly stilted, not excepting Dirk Bogarde in a hopelessly half-developed role in which he occasionally gives a twitch of his cheek to show that he has a mordant sense of humour or a twitch at the corner of his mouth to indicate buried moral scruples.' Pauline Kael's judgement was: 'Bogarde is a virtuoso at this civilized, stifled anguish racket.' Dirk shrugged

philosophically and returned, gratefully, to
Le Pigeonnier.

For the next two years he tended his
garden, entertained his family and friends,
rebuilt his terrace and made no films at all.
He did, however, begin to think about his
childhood, the last truly idyllic time when a
house (the cottage in Sussex) had seemed to
encapsulate all he wanted from life. From
that childhood musing came *A Postillion
Struck by Lightning*, an enchanting and
beautifully written memoir of his earliest
days. This won far better reviews than he
had had for some years,
and deservedly, since he
not only wrote but also
illustrated his writing with delicate pen-and-
ink drawings of the places and people that
had populated his early life. The book is
not an autobiography in the conventional
sense — there are no dates, no chronology,
no events — yet in *A Postillion Struck by
Lightning* there is an unusual joy in
recollection that Dirk has been able to
retain throughout his seven volumes of
autobiography and five novels.

BOGARDE AS AUTHOR IN THE
MIDST OF A LONG BOOK TOUR.

11 <u>DISASTER</u>

'But our life is not really in the control of players at all, it is in the control of the Director.'

Dirk was coaxed back to the cinema by the usual mixture of poverty and interest. For almost fifteen years he and the great French director Alain Resnais had been trying to find a film to do together; what they finally arrived at, in 1977, was *Providence*, Resnais' first film in English, with a complicated screenplay by David Mercer. The central premise is that of a dying author (John Gielgud in the role Dirk had really wanted for himself) who spends his last night on earth casting his own family as the characters in his latest novel. As a result of this highly complex structure — the narrative is constantly interrupted by flashbacks and memories and nightmares — the audience is very hard pressed to work out what is real and what is fantasy.

Dirk himself had no such problem. For him, *Providence* allowed the kind of 'total-immersion' acting he likes best. 'I was playing two different people. I was playing the real man at the very end of the film and my father's imagination of me in one part and in the third part, because there were three parts, his imagination translated to the novels which he was thinking about in his head. So, you try that for size. You try and ask a student to even do one of those things. You can't do it unless you are totally and utterly prepared to be dedicated and give it all up and you are possessed, silly as it may seem, because it's re-representing, regurgitating somebody else entirely, from the way he would cut his toenails

WITH DIRECTOR ALAIN RESNAIS OFF THE SET OF HIS 1977 MOVIE *PROVIDENCE*.

AN ALL-STAR CAST FOR
PROVIDENCE: BOGARDE WITH
SIR JOHN GIELGUD, ELLEN
BURSTYN AND DAVID WARNER.

to the way he picks his nose and it's got to be "on the nail" always, otherwise an audience is going to watch you acting but they are not going to identify.'

John Gielgud found it 'by far the most exciting film I have ever made' and apart from him and Dirk, there were only three other actors involved: Ellen Burstyn, David Warner and Elaine Stritch. 'Here we are all together,' Dirk said to Gielgud one day on the set, 'in some extraordinary part of France. After all the time we have both spent on our various careers, we are both now ageing gentlemen, both in a new script written specifically for us by David Mercer,

both in a new form of an old craft. We are both going ahead, that's what's exciting. At least we're not doing a revival of *No, No, Nanette*.' Dirk, although he was playing the son rather than the father, relished the chance to work with Gielgud and with another really titanic director. His work has always been characterized by the intelligence to know what a director wanted from him and his ability to work with different directors in the way that was best for them and not, incidentally, also for Bogarde. Dirk says he liked them all. 'I have never worked with a director I didn't like. I have sometimes worked with a director I didn't terribly respect but that's *force majeure* if you've got to do three movies a year anyway, whether you like them or not. You can't be choosy but from my point of view it has to be like marriage. More than a marriage, because marriages are not always love affairs. It's got to be a love affair and it's got to last. It is a total giving of your physical body, your mind and your trust to some other person and it's very hard to find those people, but if you do find them, never let them go. It's not a carnal thing — you can have a love affair without carnality. It is a lot to do with respect and respect for somebody's mind and intellect that is higher, by far, than one's own.'

The reviews for Gielgud were ecstatic — after all, it is not very often that you get to see the greatest actor of the century stuffing pessaries up his backside — but for Dirk they were less than enthusiastic. Pauline Kael, never a fan, wondered in the *New Yorker* 'how anyone can distinguish between Dirk Bogarde acting arch and just acting as usual', while in the *Sunday Times*, Alan Brien found him 'all brisk crackle and pop, dry as toast and twice as brittle, like a middle-

aged juvenile in a weekly rep rehearsal of a very minor Noël Coward'.

Dirk's luck in movies was now running very low indeed. Given his natural reticence and his wariness of the press, it's hard to tell how much he cared about the fate of his industry, especially now that he had discovered a new career as a writer. He

GIELGUD AND BOGARDE IN THEIR ONLY SIGNIFICANT SCREEN ENCOUNTER.

A Bridge Too Far: 'As portrayed by Dirk Bogarde this General is not one I would have trusted to run a cocktail party' (*Daily Telegraph*).

loved, indeed loves still, the ability to work alone, the lack of necessity for an entire army of supporting staff operating bits of incomprehensible equipment: catering trucks, wardrobe vans and the like. Now he was able to sit in his own beloved home with a friendly sheet of paper and work at his own pace. Films had not so much passed him by as used him up, but his five novels from *A Gentle Occupation* to *A Period of Adjustment* fill a shelf with gentle cynicism, astute observation, wry humour and a sense of place which is rare among today's 'literary' novelists.

And then, just to prove that no good deed goes unpunished, there was the furore over the Second World War epic *A Bridge Too Far*. This was the 1977 all-star account of the Battle of Arnhem and, again as a favour to Richard Attenborough, Dirk accepted the role of Sir Frederick 'Boy' Browning, the general who commanded the airborne troops and was seen in the film to ignore some crucial intelligence about the Germans' power.

No sooner had Dirk's casting been announced than Browning's widow, the novelist Daphne du Maurier, told the *Daily Express* that he was completely wrong for the part: 'My husband was elegant and fastidious but never effete.' When the film was released, its own military adviser, General Sir John Hackett, wrote to *The Times* complaining that Dirk's portrayal of Browning as a superficial, heartless and flippant officer was 'untruthful, unkind,

wounding and offensive. The portrayal of "Boy" Browning is the outstanding blot in an otherwise generally fair picture.' And it was Dame Daphne who had the last word: 'My God, they would not have dared to do this if "Boy" had still been alive. He would have roasted them.' And it was left to the critic of the *Daily Telegraph* to comment that Bogarde's General 'is not one I would have trusted to run a cocktail party'.

It was time for another Gallic shrug and another graceful retreat to Le Pigeonnier and the typewriter. The second in the sequence of seven autobiographies, *Snakes and Ladders*, was now well under way and,

although there had been a plan for him to film *Under the Volcano*, in the role that eventually went to Albert Finney, that fell through because of the instability of the Mexican government. Therefore Dirk was, quite happily, at a loose end.

When the phone finally rang, it was Tom Stoppard, whom he had never met, announcing that he had just finished a screenplay of Nabokov's *Despair*, which was to be directed in Germany by Rainer Werner Fassbinder, the brilliant but highly

'A TWITCHILY NEUROTIC PERFORMANCE BY DIRK BOGARDE AT HIS MOST UNINGRATIATING' (*OBSERVER*). THE TWIN MOUSTACHE BELONGS TO SEAN CONNERY IN *A BRIDGE TOO FAR* (1977).

unstable German director. Although his mother had been a German-English interpreter, Fassbinder started his first English-language film by refusing to speak English at all until Dirk, realizing he understood him perfectly well, threatened to quit. Then it became clear to Dirk that, combined with his co-stars' *mélange* of accents, his Home Counties enunciation wouldn't do at all, so his interpreter was pressed into service to find something more suitable. What he came up with, for this story of a schizophrenic businessman on the eve of the Third Reich, was Prussian, and Dirk used it throughout his tortured role as Hermann, the cuckold, who becomes convinced that a tramp is his double and kills him in order to assume his identity.

Fassbinder's encyclopaedic knowledge of film history and his own disturbed state — he

WITH BERNHARD WICKI AND THE DIRECTOR RAINER WERNER FASSBINDER ON LOCATION FOR *DESPAIR* (1978).

killed himself in 1982, after admitting that *Despair* was his suicide note — allowed him to pay homage to a number of other directors, from Billy Wilder to Orson Welles. With a literate Stoppard script and a director who, although mad, was, many believe, a genius, Dirk had a wonderful time despite the discomforts of the locations and Fassbinder's insistence on working amid loud and incessant noise. While it was happening Dirk was convinced, as he wrote in *An Orderly Man*, 'that things were going better than well and Rainer had never been seen to ... show such evident signs of pleasure'. It was, he believed, the best screen performance he had ever given. On his last day, Fassbinder thanked Dirk for showing him how to combine authority with freedom instead of fear. They parted on the best possible terms. 'When I finally finished with Fassbinder and I saw the

'BOGARDE CATCHES THE FASTIDIOUSLY DETACHED ASPECT OF THE CHARACTER BUT SIGNALS THE INNER STRESS A LITTLE TOO POWERFULLY THROUGH THAT NOW FAMOUS TWITCH AND THAT FAMILIAR LIP-FINGERING MOTION' (*OBSERVER*).

cut of *Despair* … in Paris, where we had some extra dialogue lines, I saw it in black and white and it was absolutely, staggeringly magical, the whole film.'

There was a year between the end of the shoot and the Cannes Film Festival, at which *Despair* was the official German entry. Dirk was tipped for the Best Actor award and the film itself, on the basis of the rough cut Dirk had seen and which had been widely circulated, the favourite to win the Palme d'Or. But in the event the title proved

prophetic. On the day of the screening Dirk descended into Cannes and was intercepted on the terrace of the Carlton Hotel by the cinematographer, who begged him not to attend. Highly distressed, the man described a film cut to ribbons by its self-destructive director so that Dirk's role no longer made sense and his co-star, the spunky Andréa Ferréol, who played his wife, no longer had a role at all.

So Dirk and Andréa had to sit through the film they had made, decimated by Fassbinder's final cut, and to face the press immediately afterwards. 'Well, we had to go out of duty to the press. It was a terrific thing, a Fassbinder first night and the first time he'd worked with professional actors: Andréa and me. I made him come down and he came down and he behaved appallingly and looked so stupid. I'm saying all these things about a man I absolutely revered and he's dead now, so I can say it — I wouldn't otherwise. He was a genius and I say that quite calmly and clearly. He was a genius and geniuses are notoriously loony because it is a very fine line between madness and genius. But he'd taken whatever pills he took, and in a dirty black T-shirt he insulted the press, insulted us all and he said the film was a message for his suicide. Well, I knew more than they did that he was telling the truth, but the point was that I felt everything I ever had draining out of me. Sitting there at the press conference with all the lights on and all these idiots waiting with questions poised, from every newspaper in the whole world there, Andréa sitting icily beside me, despairing because her performance had been wrecked and mine had been fucked up anyway and I just thought, No. Go back to the farm — because I was only up the mountain about forty-five minutes away — and never come back.'

He went, and didn't come back to the cinema for twelve years.

BOGARDE (HERE WITH KLAUS LOWITSCH AS FELIX) 'GIVES HIS USUAL STAUNCH PERFORMANCE IN A ROTTEN ROLE' (NEW STATESMAN).

12 LOOKING BACK

'I was filled with eager curiosity about working in Hollywood once again, now that I had reached the sensible, balanced age of sixty.'

There was bound to be a limit to the time Dirk could go on playing Timon of the movies in the seclusion of his French farm. As usual, everything still had to be paid for and by 1981, barely three years after *Despair* and his declaration of independence, he was back in front of the cameras, in Hollywood for the first time since *Justine*, twelve years earlier.

But this was television — an adaptation of Barry Farrell's *Pat and Roald*, a biography of Roald Dahl and his wife, the distinguished actress Patricia Neal, whose valiant fight to regain her life and career after a crippling stroke was the stuff of which drama is made.

On paper, the omens were all good. Dirk was to play Roald Dahl and his co-star as Patricia Neal was to be Glenda Jackson, an actress whose work he had always admired. In addition, he knew the Dahls, having been a neighbour in Buckinghamshire many years earlier. In the event, almost everything that could go wrong did so almost immediately. The first plan was to release *Pat and Roald* for television in America but as a film for the cinema in the rest of the world. This led to arguments about which medium should be given precedence, and the television people won every battle. It was they who then demanded that about a third of the script be cut and the title changed to

LIFE *À LA PROVENÇALE*: AT HOME IN THE IDYLLIC YEARS OF LE PIGEONNIER.

The Patricia Neal Story. Then there were further rows about where to put the commercial breaks and Dirk realized that his dream of getting a film release was simply unrealistic. Halfway through shooting, the unit moved back to England but, as the director Anthony Harvey had other commitments in Hollywood, a new director, Anthony Page, was hired to pick up the pieces.

This was in many ways, however, a happy experience for Dirk, because he found working with Glenda Jackson 'one of the highlights of my life. On the *Patricia Neal Story* the American crew were fascinated because we never left the set. I remember Glenda preparing, just for a moment, for a long, long take with me and she went to the corner, said she was OK. Then she put down her head, I could see her eyes were closed and her body began to force — it was the most extraordinary sight to see. Nothing really happened but she seemed to swell in this passion and then she just said, "OK" and went. But if you touched her, I promise you, she would have exploded into shattered bits because the concentration was so intense.'

In giving up the theatre all those years ago Dirk had denied himself the opportunity of working with a whole new generation of stage talent; of that generation Glenda was one of the outstanding examples and, in any case, he has always been fascinated by and generous to really good actors. 'I've had a catalytic effect on the careers of a lot of players — Michael York, James Fox, Sarah Miles, Julie Christie

THE ACTOR TURNS AUTHOR:
DIRK AT THE BEGINNING OF HIS
SECOND BOOK TOUR.

BACK HOME IN FRANCE FOR HIS
LAST YEARS ON THE FARM.

and Charlotte Rampling. Now they've gone off like rockets into space and you can't even see them.'

Part of Dirk's pride in his influence on others is his highly developed consciousness of the techniques he himself has learned. 'You are half dead at the end of the day's shoot. You have to observe because you have to see what people do. I mean you are always representing some other person. I've never played myself in my life on the screen, so I've got to look at people and see how they do it. How do they pick up a cup? How are you left-handed? How do you write a letter with your left hand? There are other imbalances as well, not just left-handing. So you've got to watch those things and I've seen it myself actually — even in intense grief and despair I've caught my face in a mirror and through the misery and despair and probably tears, I've often looked up and thought, Oh, so that's what I do. That's how it happens. That's how I look. Part of that mechanism up there is still ticking over in the most obscene manner. I am still collecting and observing.'

When the film was completed there was a euphoric moment at which the theory was that Emmys, the television Oscars, would go to both Dirk and Glenda and that it still wasn't too late for a theatrical release, after all. But those dreams died again when the ratings came in at less than fifty per cent. By the uncomfortable element of chance that has so often beset Dirk's career, the low ratings for *The Patricia Neal Story* were less about the inadequacies of that programme than about the interest America showed in Robert Wagner. As

THE 1980 GUARDIAN LECTURE AT THE NATIONAL FILM THEATRE.

fate would have it, this was the week
Natalie Wood had died in a mysterious
boating accident and America wanted to see
how her husband, starring in *Hart to Hart*
on the other channel, was taking it.

All the same, *The Patricia Neal Story* did
seem to have a curious curse on it. It was
during the shooting that Pat and Roald,
who had survived such domestic drama,
decided to end their marriage. This may, of
course, have been one of the reasons they
had objected so strongly to the making of
the film in the first place.

Five years were to elapse before Dirk's

next appearance on camera, this time in his
own adaptation of the Graham Greene
short story *May We Borrow Your
Husband?* A young husband is hotly
pursued by a number of guests in his
honeymoon hotel, most of them male, while
Charlotte Attenborough, as his impossibly
naive wife, is more coolly if implausibly
pursued by Dirk's character, a novelist
staying at the same hotel. As the critic
Robert Tanich pointed out, 'Bogarde's
screenplay took Greene's short story far too
seriously, turning what was a cynical
Somerset Maughamish comedy of sexual

bad manners into a mini-tragedy of unrequited love ... His performance, however, was remarkable (as always) for the range of emotion his face could convey in close-up without the help of any dialogue.'

But in the meantime Dirk was not exactly idle. There was always the land around Le Pigeonnier to satisfy his rustic inclinations and he was now, with absolute justification, describing himself as 'an author who sometimes acts'. In a very short space of time, thanks to the enthusiasm and education he was receiving from his editor and publisher, the late and remarkable Nora

Smallwood at Chatto, he had effectively invented a whole new style of star autobiography. *A Postillion Struck by Lightning* had become an immediate bestseller, as had *Snakes and Ladders* and now *An Orderly Man*. There were still four more volumes left to go in that sequence, plus five novels and a volume of correspondence, but what was fascinating in the memoirs was a radical difference in tone from that of any other autobiographies by contemporary actors.

The last (and almost the only) great

REUNION WITH AVA GARDNER TWENTY-FIVE YEARS AFTER *THE ANGEL WORE RED*.

bestsellers by an actor had been those of David Niven a decade earlier, but where they were effectively anthologies of all the best Hollywood anecdotes that anybody had ever told him, Dirk's were the work of a novelist, and a literary novelist at that. It's not that they weren't entirely true, but that they are shot through with a kind of poetic melancholy and an extraordinary degree of self-knowledge. Few names are ever dropped, and many of his films never even rate a mention. These seven volumes taken together add up unquestionably, in my view, to the most honest insight into how an actor works and how a man learns to live with his own demons. The novels are almost elegiac in their search for lost loves and worlds which never really existed. His South of France in *Jericho*, for instance, is a magic place, coloured certainly by his love for Le Pigeonnier, but it is also a yearning for a kind of home that Dirk himself found only twice — in the Sussex of his childhood and the Grasse of his long exile.

'I took over a shed in the garden, installed my old electric typewriter and stacked the shelves with every reference book I could possibly need. Then I locked the door. No one was allowed to come inside. I clocked in every morning at 8.30 and worked through until midday, whatever happened. Then I went back for another couple of hours every evening. That shed was my womb, where my real life was lived, and here the books got written.'

His only serious error as a writer was to print his address at the end of his first chapter of autobiography. 'The result was

that quite ghastly people would appear on my doorstep unannounced and all clamouring for an autograph.'

Professionally, the mid-1980s were a good time for Dirk. Admittedly he had not had a film offer from his native country for twenty years but the French gave him the Chevalier de l'Ordre des Arts et des Lettres in 1982 and three years later he received an honorary Doctorate of Letters from St Andrews University in Scotland. In 1984 he received an honour previously unheard of by the British, when he was asked to preside over the Cannes Film Festival Jury. He repaid the debt by making sure, that year at least, that the American movie invaders went home empty-handed. Throughout Europe, moreover, he was revered as one of the very few Englishmen who had put his career into Continental hands. He was now making enough out of his publishing royalties not to have to worry, as always in the past, about where the next film was coming from.

But privately, this was the worst of times. His mother had died just before his sixtieth birthday in 1981 at a private hotel ('not a home', she insisted) in Brighton. It was there that his exhausted sister had finally put their mother when her drinking and her increasing frailty converged at the house they had shared and she was discovered, after Elizabeth's short absence, at the bottom of the stairs with every bone in her body broken except, as Dirk noted, her neck. Theirs had never been a relationship made in heaven — it was Ulric he loved — but she was his mother and he mourned not

only what she had been but what she could
have been.

And there was yet worse still to come. In
1983 Tony Forwood was diagnosed as
suffering from a lethal combination of
cancer and Parkinson's disease. They
managed to hold out at Le Pigeonnier for
three more years, but with Dirk unable to
drive and Forwood now frequently too tired
to carry out all his usual tasks for them
both, a shadow now fell on their home. It
was only a matter of time before they
would have to leave the only place where
they had both been truly happy.

But while Forwood was still well enough
to be left alone Dirk returned to London to
make a BBC Television film called *The
Vision*. A decade ahead of its time, it was a
satirical drama about the days of
evangelical television channels and Dirk was
given two hugely distinguished co-stars in
Lee Remick and Eileen Atkins, with the
young Helena Bonham-Carter playing his
daughter. In many ways *The Vision*
resembled *Network*, a film Peter Finch had
made twelve years earlier, only this time
Dirk's ageing newscaster was having an
affair with a communist spy (female) while
secretly homosexual. *The Vision* marked
Dirk's first return to the BBC in forty years
but, with the success of his early memoirs,
he would now take to the chat-show circuit
whenever he had a book to sell, still
complaining bitterly about the invasion of
his privacy which these appearances
involved.

On his return to France, Dirk realized
that Forwood could no longer be left alone

and, worse, that they would have to come
back to England to be close to both the
necessary medical facilities and their
families. He had to turn down the one good
film offer that came his way and might have
brought him back to cinematic prominence.
David Puttnam offered him the lead in *The
Mission*, a role that went instead to Jeremy
Irons, on a location picture set in South
America. By this time, Forwood was very ill
and the living in the countryside was
becoming increasingly impossible. Dirk's
own writing describes, better than anyone
else could, his desolation
at leaving Le Pigeonnier,
and he has both talked

ON THE ROAD AT THE START
OF YET ANOTHER BOOK TOUR.

and written at length about losing his home, a loss as real as the loss of his friend. Their first plan had been to move to Paris but Dirk knew he would never be able to write there and instead they took a tiny house in Kensington. Dirk hated it after the unfussy space they had been used to, but it pleased Forwood and that was enough for Dirk, even when in November 1987 he suffered a slight stroke on the stairs.

A few months later Forwood died with all the grace and dignity that had been the hallmark of his life. His son made the funeral arrangements and Dirk was, truly, for the first time in his adult life, on his own. His devotion to Forwood over more than forty years left him bereft after the funeral and in this terrible time he was not helped by a story in the *News of the World* that tried to suggest that Forwood had died of AIDS. This set up in Dirk a deep and understandable loathing of the British press, but in one of the many contradictions that make up his life story it was about now that he himself started to work as a journalist. Not only did he begin regularly reviewing books for the *Sunday Telegraph*, but he also produced wonderfully waspish articles

WITH THE LATE LEE REMICK IN *THE VISION*, NORMAN STONE'S 1988 TELEVISION FILM ABOUT THE DANGERS OF TELEVISION ITSELF.

about the sheer bloody awfulness of London dinner parties, after the publication of which, typically, he would complain that nobody seemed to ask him out any more. He was also contributing random pieces on travel and gardening and when *The Times* was celebrating its bicentenary he wrote a loving account of Ulric as the first Art Editor, thereby at last realizing his late father's dream that they should both work for that newspaper.

He had bought a flat just off Sloane Square, characteristically only a few hundred yards from one of his very first homes. 'I was glad to be back in Chelsea, where I had lived as an art student at the Chelsea Poly in 1938, taught by Graham Sutherland. Years and years later, I asked

Graham if he'd paint me but he refused because he said my face had not got any character. Which was news to me.' On his doctor's orders, he chose a block with a resident porter in case he had another stroke.

Very tentatively, Dirk was now working his way back towards the theatre, although not, of course, to a play. He had started at the National Theatre, giving platform performances of a show about Saki, and on the book tours he now ventured beyond interviews to a kind

of one-man show about his life and work. He had also discovered the joys of BBC Radio, for which, in the early 1990s, he not only read most of his own books but also narrated a production of *The Forsyte Saga* and some stories by Somerset Maugham, and even recorded Pinter's *No Man's Land* in the role originally played by Sir John Gielgud.

As far as he could see, his life in films was entirely over: 'Casting directors nowadays are all about twelve and they keep asking my agent to send in a video so they can see what I look like.' But suddenly,

just when it seemed there would never be another appearance before the cameras, there was even the possibility of another movie on the horizon.

Dirk was typically bullish about it. 'I'm seventy and completely happy where I am. I've got the books I have written which have made the bestseller lists, a flat with a view over London, I've recovered from a stroke and after twelve years of nothing I have got a film I am pleased to put my name to.'

OPPOSITE: A LIFETIME ACHIEVEMENT AWARD FROM BAFTA IN 1988.
ABOVE: WITH JEAN SIMMONS AT THE BAFTA AWARDS.

13 A DIGNIFIED EXIT

'I thought if you can be in that kind of film ... you can go out on that, honey, and not on a ruined film with the unfortunate title of Despair.'

What eventually brought Dirk back to the movies was a combination of a challenge and the chance to work with Bertrand Tavernier, a big bear of a director with a shock of white hair and fluent English, who had been Joseph Losey's press agent. The challenge was in wresting the role of the father in *Daddy Nostalgie* from two other actors, Denholm Elliott and Peter O'Toole, both high on Tavernier's wish list. The script had been sent to Bogarde about halfway through his self-imposed retirement in France and he had hated it, not least because it was written for an eighty-year-old man. Dirk's vanity was, thank goodness, still in place.

Several years later Dirk heard that Jane Birkin was working on a new film with Tavernier and had been asked to help locate an actor to play her father. Rather than provide her with Peter O'Toole's private number, Dirk established that the film was *Daddy Nostalgie*, now being directed by a man he badly wanted to work with, and, as he says: 'I made a bid ... I got rid of the other guy.'

This was one of Dirk's leaps of faith that turned out to be exactly what he'd hoped for. 'It was a total love affair and it was an instinctive thing on my part.' He wanted to play a man he had written himself. 'I just changed things to fit my mouth

WITH JANE BIRKIN IN 1990, ON THE SET OF *THESE FOOLISH THINGS* (*DADDY NOSTALGIE*).

[because] Tavernier and I agreed that he was rather a common little man really, in his manner, in his rudeness, in his lack of concern for that daughter and he would brag that he had been a very important part of Yardley's when, in actual fact, all he was was a commercial traveller. But he had fantasies. So I changed things around and made him a bit of a shit, but one that you liked. So I had the chance of doing my onion-skin act, in so far as I think that any part I ever play is like an onion. You peel the skin off layer by layer by layer by layer for ever until you find the little nub right in the middle. I find they're fun to do and very often an audience finds that an intriguing system to watch. So, I was putting all those things into *Daddy Nostalgie*, from the clothes downwards. Bertrand was with me. Those awful shoes that I bought from Clark's, a terrible old jacket and things, all

my own gear. I mean I walked around like a living bundle for Oxfam.'

Tavernier used him as a touchstone, as a writer, as a father figure. 'When the film was finally finished, I was in bed back here with flu and Bertrand called up and he said, "We've seen the first cut but it lacks one scene. Towards the end of the film, which is not right yet ... between you and Jane." And I said, "What's that going to be?" and he said, "You must talk to your daughter about death and pain and dying and your life," and I said, "Bertrand, I can't do all that. I'm in bed with flu, I've got a temperature of 103 and you cannot intellectualize pain. It's not a metaphorical thing. It's like a bad neighbour ..." and Bertrand shouted over the line from Paris, "Write that!" So I wrote it.

'[Tavernier] rewrote a lot of that himself because he had his own point of view on death, because his own father had also just died and it had distressed him greatly because he was very close to his father. Forwood had also died within the year, so I'd been nursing a dying man for a bit and we both knew what terminal pain was like and we knew what caring for it was like, so it did give it a certain validity. One could really write from true experience without being arty-farty about it and I think that final scene was the clincher for *Daddy Nostalgie* and then Bertrand did one of those

magical things. We'd finished the shoot and I was going. He said, "One thing, I've just had an idea. Would you just do a couple of lines? Anything you can think of, we can put it on the answering machine of Jane's telephone and she'll use it at the very end of the film and it can just be the last thing you say to her because ..." So I said, "You mean he's going to kill himself?" and he said, "Yes, I think so. After that scene I think he hasn't got long and he must know that. You made that clear to the audience. We've done that scene." So I just said to the mike, in the studio: "It's Daddy calling ... whatever I say, I can't remember and there's no message,

nothing to say — just, 'I love you.'" Well, that absolutely broke everyone up, broke me up now. But that is the brilliance of someone like Bertrand, who has exactly the precise recipe to end a film with, which, I thought, in my way, was a salutary farewell to the cinema.'

In his most recent television interview Dirk was asked whether this was the beginning of a late-life revival in films. 'No. I've no intention of coming back but everything has been fun. They've always been fun.'

THESE FOOLISH THINGS, HIS LAST FILM TO DATE – 'A MINIATURE JEWEL OF A FILM, ACTED AND DIRECTED WITH BRILLIANT SUBTLETY' (*VARIETY*).

Daddy Nostalgie was retitled *These Foolish Things* for England and America, thereby making it sound like a 1930s Hollywood musical. Watching it, wrote George Perry in the *Sunday Times*, 'is to be aware of the loss to British cinema since Bogarde's departure in frustration more than twenty years ago', and if this was to be his last film (he has certainly made no other in the past five years) then indeed it was a farewell with both dignity and elegance. Settled back in his Chelsea flat, Dirk worked on two new novels, *West of Sunset* and *Jericho*, and turned his first, *Voices in the Garden*, into a television play. Early in 1992 he was knighted for services to the cinema, an honour he was initially disinclined to accept and then, at the last minute, agreed to because he knew his father would have been so proud of him. Characteristically, he spent much of the Investiture worrying about where the nearest Palace bathroom could be located.

A distinct irritability is now the keynote of most public appearances. When BAFTA (British Academy of Film and Television Arts) gave him its highest honour, a Life Achievement Award, he was more than slightly unappreciative. In his acceptance speech he bitched publicly about the film fans who had destroyed his stage career and, commenting on the death of director Charles Vidor three weeks into the filming of *Song without End*, he said, 'It did not distress any of us greatly.'

He is still to be found, as often as not, pottering around the area of Chelsea bordered by the King's Road and Sloane Street like some increasingly tetchy old tortoise, forever challenging journalists to winkle him out of his shell and knowing that they will always fail. He has written his memoirs as if they were novels and the last two are shot through with the melancholy metaphor of a lovingly constructed sandcastle being destroyed by the tide. But these books are full of curious contradictions: few men with such an angry passion for their own privacy and anonymity actually write seven volumes of memoirs and then take to the stage of the National Theatre to read them aloud, something he had already done on audio cassettes and would go on to do on BBC Radio 4. The sound here is always of closet doors being cautiously half-opened and then slammed in our faces just as we're about to poke around inside; but the old wizard has always known enough about his large and loyal readership to understand that it is precisely the mystery that sells the books. Expecting to learn the final truth about Dirk anywhere in his own writing would be like expecting the conjurer to show us the bottom of the rabbit's hat.

And there was one last great controversy still to be fought. Early in 1991, both in print and on radio, Dirk came out in favour of voluntary euthanasia. Soon afterwards he became Vice President of the Voluntary Euthanasia Society. He wrote a 'living will', asking his doctors to end his life should he become terminally ill or mentally incompetent. He asked that his family should then sprinkle his ashes over France. His feelings, he said, had been strongly influenced by witnessing Forwood's slow and painful death but, predictably, this brought out of the woodwork all the religious do-gooders who regard his attitude to death as ungodly. Very soon he had received more than 500 letters on one side or the other. Once again, a supposedly private man found himself unwillingly in the limelight.

One of the central contradictions of Dirk's public and private life is this: he once wrote that 'an obsessional privacy has stopped me reaching the highest peak of my profession' and yet, if you are prepared to read between the lines of his books, you will find that few actors of our time have been so unashamedly self-revelatory. And he seems entirely unable to stop himself becoming

involved in battles of one kind or another. Joseph Losey, Dirk's favourite director, once said, 'He is kind, loyal, involved; gifted in many ways, as a painter, as an actor, and as a writer. Conversely, he can be cruel, though never mean; cutting but usually only when hurt himself; paranoid like all of us in this competitive jungle. Dirk always fought the system and he carries its scars.'

But Bogarde has earned the final word. 'I am alone but not lonely. I love being on my own. I am self-sufficient and rather smug about it. I think to be lonely must be one of the most terrible things ... I tend to go around my family sorting everybody out. Loneliness is having supper in the Ivy Restaurant surrounded by all those luvvies. I am too old to go back to living in France; now I'm just walking around Chelsea with ghosts.'

FILMOGRAPHY

FILMS

1939
Carry on George
Director: Anthony
Kimmins
EXTRA

1942
Dancing with Crime
Director: John Paddy
Carstairs
POLICEMAN

1948
Esther Waters
Director: Ian Dalrymple
and Peter Proud
WILLIAM LATCH
Quartet
Director: Harold French
GEORGE BLAND
Once a Jolly Swagman
Director: Jack Lee
BILL FOX

1949
Dear Mr Prohack
Director: Thornton
Freeland
CHARLES PROHACK
Boys in Brown
Director: Montgomery
Tully
ALFIE RAWLINGS

1950
The Blue Lamp
Director: Basil Dearden
TOM RILEY
So Long at the Fair
Director: Terence Fisher
and Anthony
Darnborough
GEORGE HATHAWAY
The Woman in Question
Director: Anthony Asquith
BOB BAKER

1951
Blackmailed
Director: Marc Allegret
STEPHEN MUNDY

1952
Hunted
Director: Charles Crichton
CHRIS LLOYD
Penny Princess
Director: Val Guest
TONY CRAIG
The Gentle Gunman
Director: Basil Dearden
MATT

1953
Appointment in London
Director: Philip Leacock
WING COMMANDER TIM
MASON
Desperate Moment
Director: Compton
Bennett
SIMON VAN HALDER

1954
They Who Dare
Director: Lewis Milestone
LIEUTENANT GRAHAM

Doctor in the House
Director: Ralph Thomas
SIMON SPARROW
The Sleeping Tiger
Director: Joseph Losey
FRANK CLEMENTS
For Better For Worse
Director: J. Lee-Thompson
TONY HOWARD
**The Sea Shall Not Have
Them**
Director: Lewis Gilbert
FLIGHT SERGEANT MACKAY

1955
Simba
Director: Brian Desmond
Hurst
ALAN HOWARD
Doctor at Sea
Director: Ralph Thomas
DR SIMON SPARROW
Cast a Dark Shadow
Director: Lewis Gilbert
EDWARD BARE

1956
The Spanish Gardener
Director: Philip Leacock
JOSÉ

1957
Ill Met By Moonlight
Director: Michael Powell
and Emeric Pressburger
MAJOR PATRICK LEIGH
FERMOR
Doctor at Large
Director: Ralph Thomas
DR SIMON SPARROW
Campbell's Kingdom
Director: Ralph Thomas
BRUCE CAMPBELL

1958
A Tale of Two Cities
Director: Ralph Thomas
SYDNEY CARTON

1959
The Doctor's Dilemma
Director: Anthony Asquith
LOUIS DUBEDAT
Libel
Director: Anthony Asquith
SIR MARK LODDON
FRANK WELNEY
NUMBER FIFTEEN

1960
Song Without End
Director: Charles Vidor
and George Cukor
FRANZ LISZT

1961
The Singer Not the Song
Director: Roy Baker
ANACLETO
La Sposa Bella
(English title: The Angel
Wore Red)
Director: Nunnally
Johnson
ARTURO CARRERA
Victim
Director: Basil Deardon
MELVILLE FARR

1962
H.M.S. Defiant
Director: Lewis Gilbert
LIEUTENANT SCOTT-PADGET
The Password is Courage
Director: Andrew L. Stone
SERGEANT-MAJOR CHARLES
COWARD
We Joined the Navy
Director: Wendy Toye
DR SIMON SPARROW
(guest appearance)

1963
The Mind Benders
Director: Basil Dearden
DR HENRY LONGMAN
I Could Go On Singing
Director: Ronald Neame
DAVID DONNE
Doctor in Distress
Director: Ralph Thomas
DR SIMON SPARROW
The Servant
Director: Joseph Losey
BARRETT

1964
Hot Enough for June
Director: Ralph Thomas
NICHOLAS WHISTLER
King and Country
Director: Joseph Losey
CAPTAIN HARGREAVES

1965
The High Bright Sun
Director: Ralph Thomas
MAJOR McGUIRE
Darling
Director: John Schlesinger
ROBERT GOLD

1966
Modesty Blaise
Director: Joseph Losey
GABRIEL

1967
Accident
Director: Joseph Losey
STEPHEN
Our Mother's House
Director: Jack Clayton
CHARLIE HOOK

1968
Sebastian
Director: David Greene
SEBASTIAN

1969
The Fixer
Director: John Frankenheimer
BIBIKOV
Justine
Director: George Cukor
PURSEWARDEN
Oh! What A Lovely War
Director: Richard
Attenborough
STEPHEN
Return to Lochabar
Director: Don Kelly
COMMENTARY
La Caduta Degli Dei
(English title, The Damned)
Director: Luchino Visconti
FRIEDRICH BRUCKMANN

1971
Morte a Venezia
(English title, Death in
Venice)
Director: Luchino Visconti
GUSTAV VON ASCHENBACH

1974
The Serpent
Director: Henri Verneuil
PHILIP BOYLE
Il Portiere di Notte
(English title, The Night
Porter)
Director: Liliana Cavani
MAX

1975
Permission to Kill
Director: Cyril Frankel
ALAN CURTIS

1977
Providence
Director: Alain Resnais
CLAUD LANGHAM
A Bridge Too Far
Director: Richard
Attenborough
LIEUTENANT GENERAL
BROWNING

1978
Despair
Director: Rainer Werner
Fassbinder
HERMANN

1991
Daddy Nostalgie
(English title, These Foolish
Things)
Director: Bertrand Tavernier
PAPA

TELEVISION

1947
Rope
BBC
CHARLES GRANILLO
Power Without Glory
BBC
CLIFF
The Case of Helvig Delbo
BBC
AN UNDERGROUND MAN

1965
Blithe Spirit
Hallmark, USA
CHARLES
The Epic That Never Was
BBC
COMMENTARY

1966
Little Moon of Alban
Hallmark, USA

1969
Upon This Rock
NBC
BONNIE PRINCE CHARLIE

1981
The Patricia Neal Story
CBS
ROALD DAHL

1986
**May We Borrow Your
Husband?**
Yorkshire
WILLIAM

1988
The Vision
BBC
JAMES MARRINER

THEATRE

1940
Cornelius
Westminster
LAWRENCE

1941
Diversion No. 2 (revue)
Wyndhams
VARIOUS
The Ghost Train
tour

1947
Power Without Glory
New Lindsay and Fortune
CLIFF

1948
For Better For Worse
Q
TONY

1949
Foxhole in the Parlour
New Lindsay
DENNIS PATTERSON
Sleep On My Shoulder
Q
SIMON

1950
The Shaughraun
Bedford
CAPTAIN MOLINEUX
Point of Departure
Lyric, Hammersmith,
Duke of York's
ORPHEUS

1952
The Vortex
Lyric, Hammersmith
NICKY LANCASTER

1955
Summertime
Apollo
ALBERTO

1958
Jezabel
Playhouse, Oxford
MARC

190

INDEX